CHRISTMAS MELODIES

for Ukulele

MELODY, TAB, LYRICS & CHORDS

ISBN 978-1-5400-5428-9

Visit Hal Leonard Online at
www.halleonard.com

Contact us:
Hal Leonard
7777 West Bluemound Road
Milwaukee, WI 53213
Email: info@halleonard.com

In Europe, contact:
Hal Leonard Europe Limited
42 Wigmore Street
Marylebone, London, W1U 2RN
Email: info@halleonardeurope.com

In Australia, contact:
Hal Leonard Australia Pty. Ltd.
4 Lentara Court
Cheltenham, Victoria, 3192 Australia
Email: info@halleonard.com.au

All I Want for Christmas Is My Two Front Teeth

Words and Music by Don Gardner

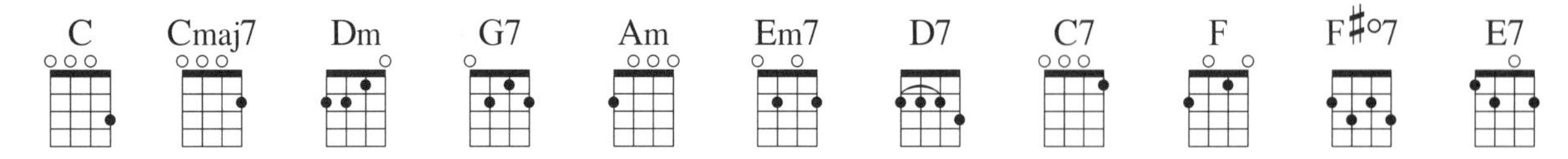

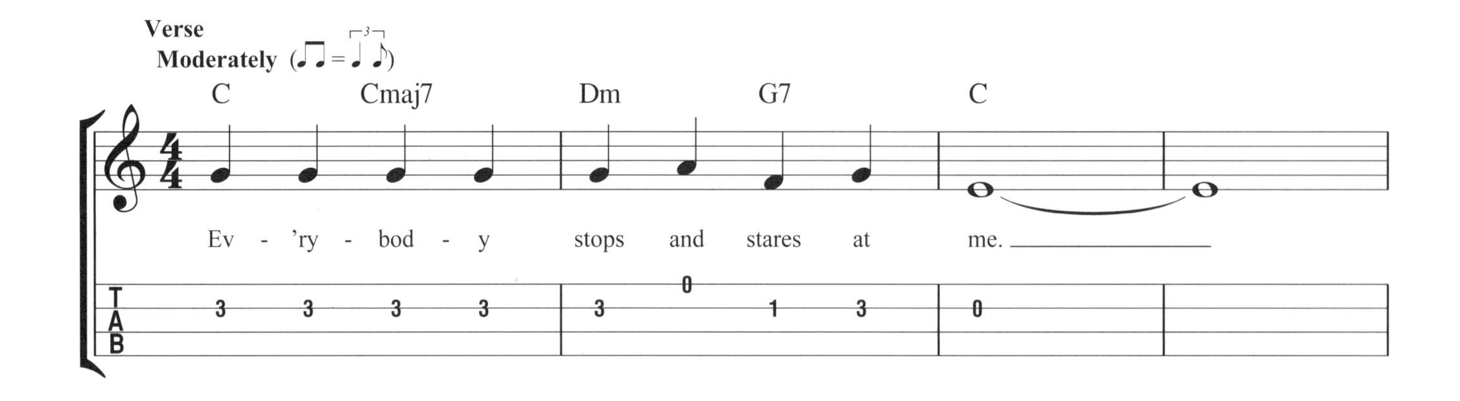

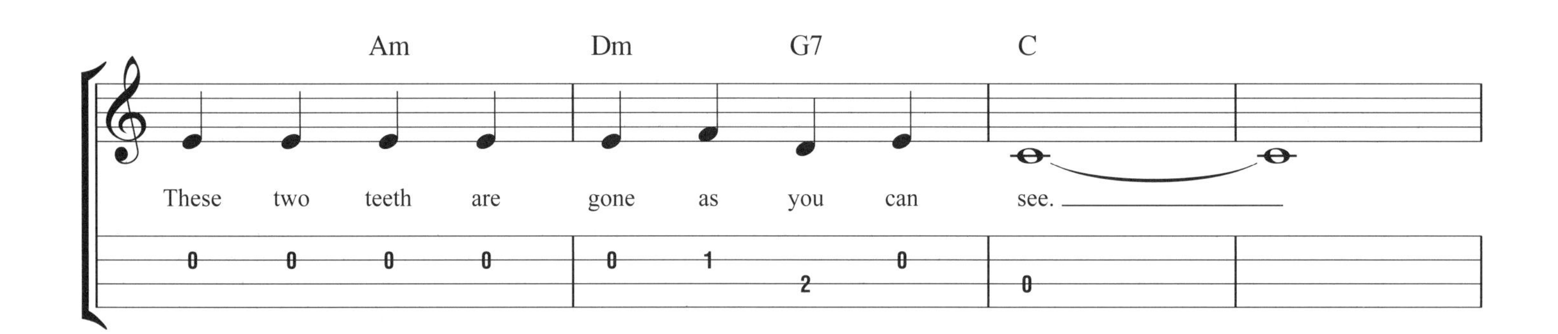

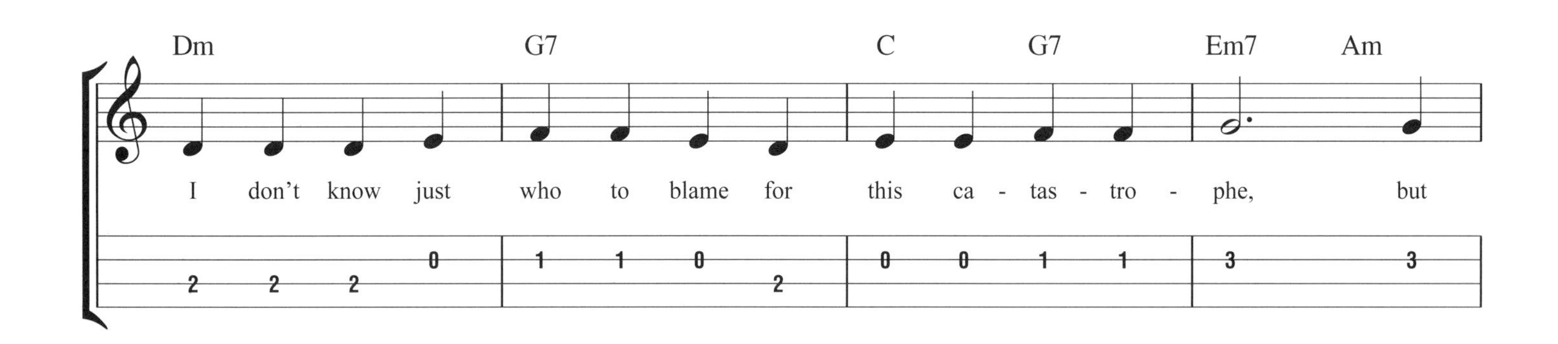

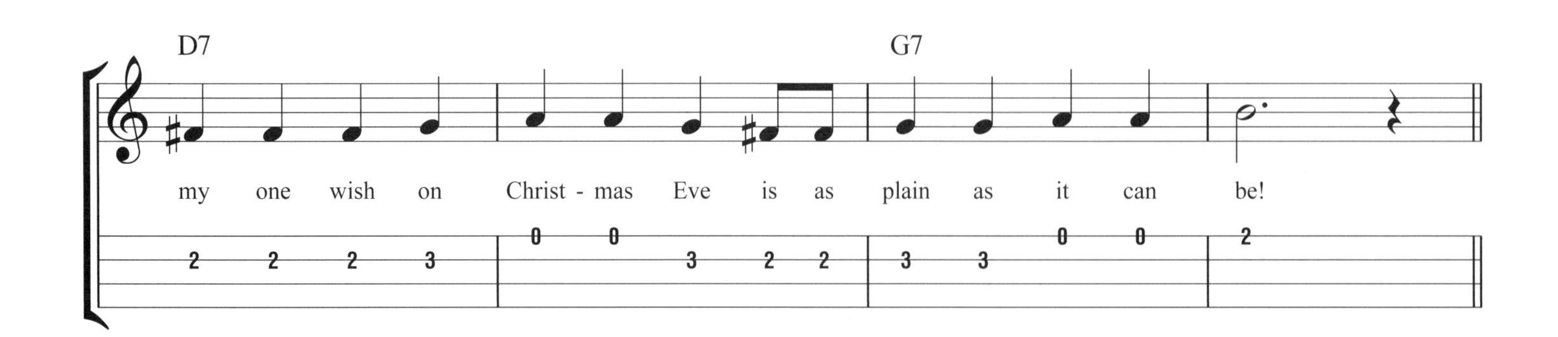

Chorus
C
D7
All I want for Christ - mas is my two front teeth, my
3 2 3 2 3 0 3 0 2 2 2 0

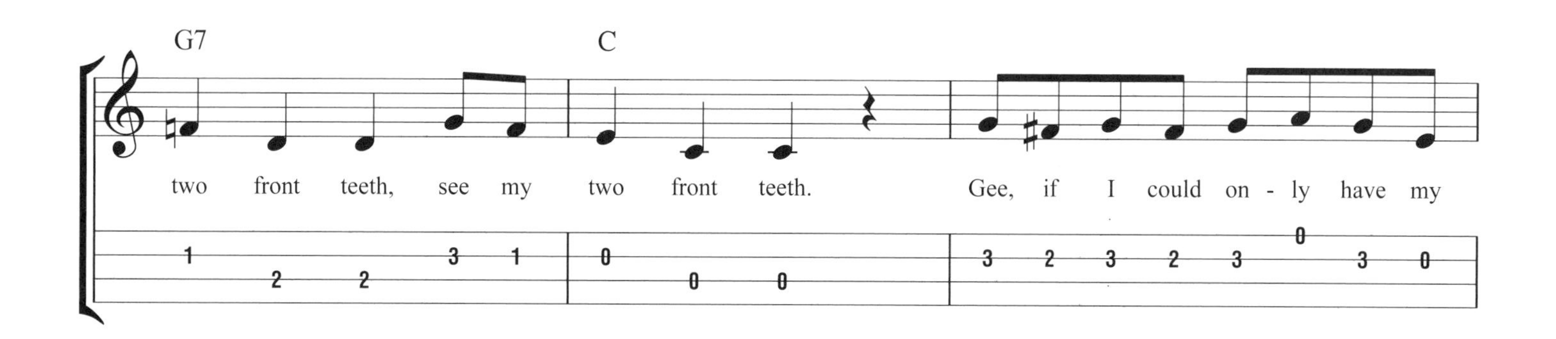
G7
C
two front teeth, see my two front teeth. Gee, if I could on - ly have my
1 2 2 3 1 0 0 0 3 2 3 2 3 0 3 0

D7
G7
two front teeth, then I could wish you "Mer - ry
2 2 2 0 1 1 1 3 0 3

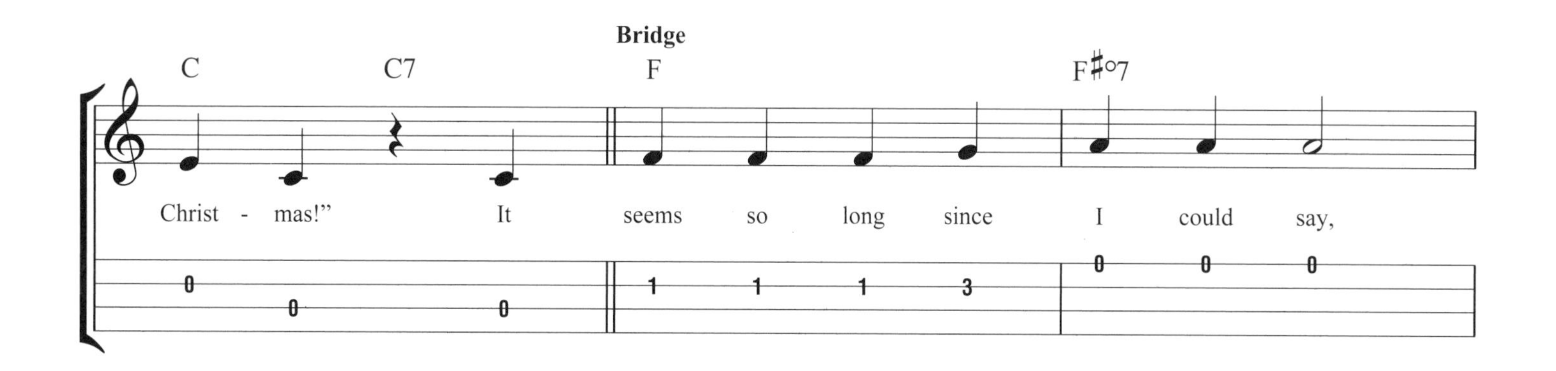
Bridge
C
C7
F
F♯°7
Christ - mas!" It seems so long since I could say,
0 0 0 1 1 1 3 0 0 0

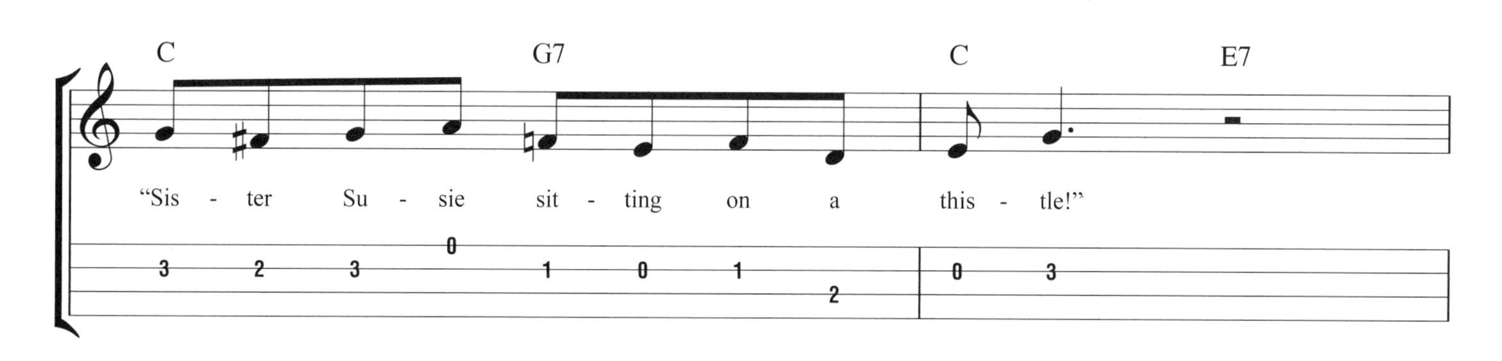
C
G7
C
E7
"Sis - ter Su - sie sit - ting on a this - tle!"
3 2 3 0 1 0 1 2 0 3

Am
D7
Gosh, oh gee, how hap - py I'd be if I could on - ly

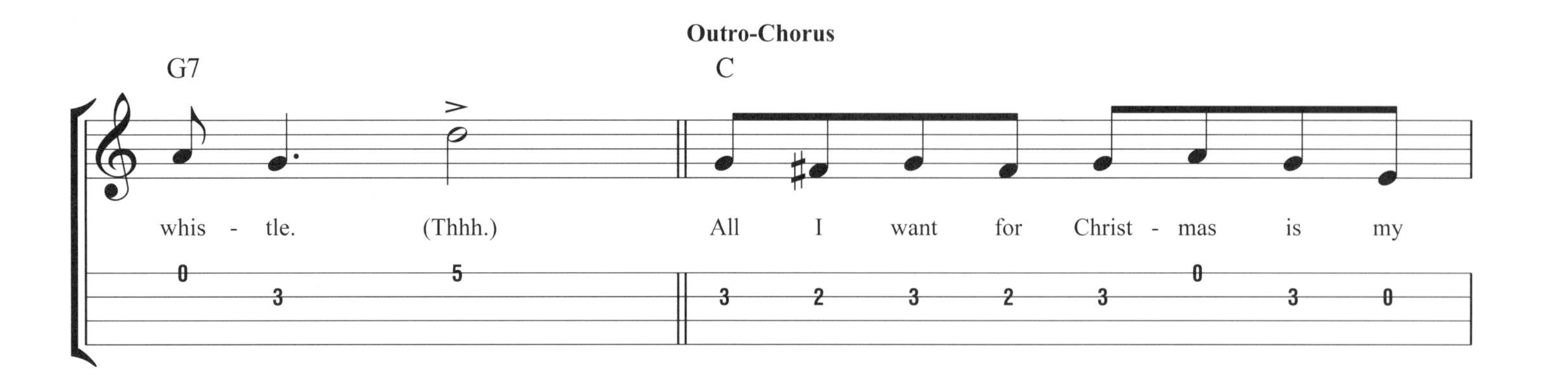
Outro-Chorus
G7
C
whis - tle. (Thhh.) All I want for Christ - mas is my

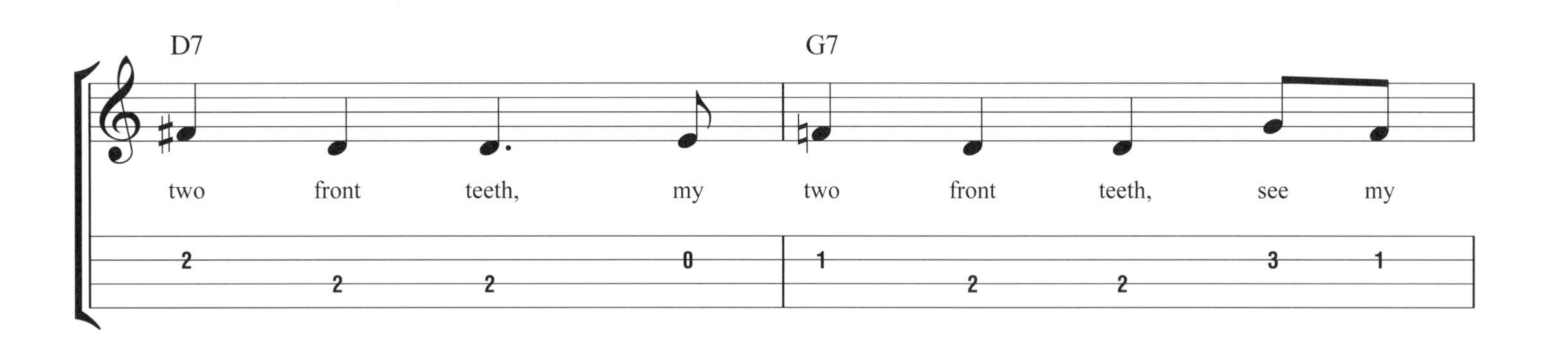
D7
G7
two front teeth, my two front teeth, see my

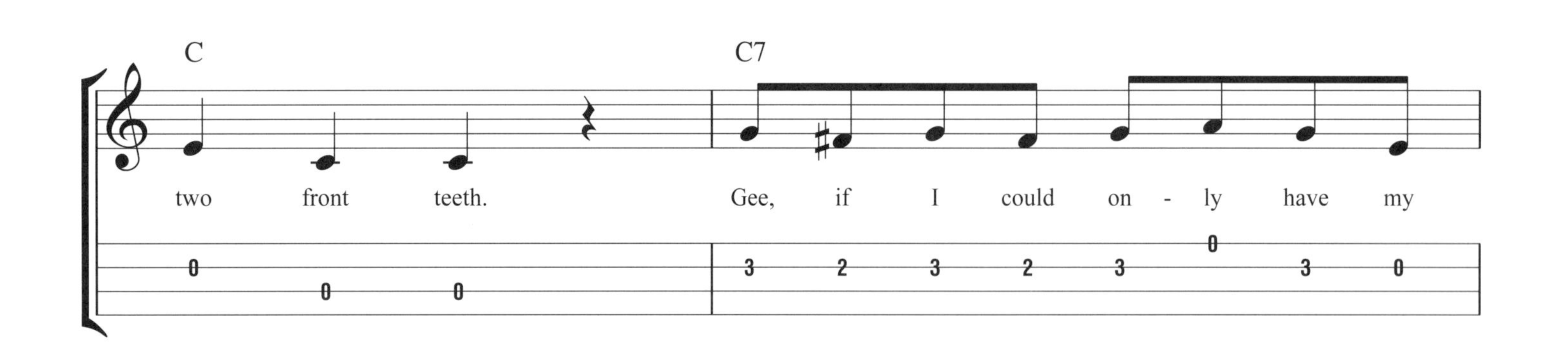
C
C7
two front teeth. Gee, if I could on - ly have my

F
F♯°7
C
G7
C
two front teeth, then I could wish you "Mer - ry Christ - mas!"

Christmas Time Is Here

from A CHARLIE BROWN CHRISTMAS

Words by Lee Mendelson
Music by Vince Guaraldi

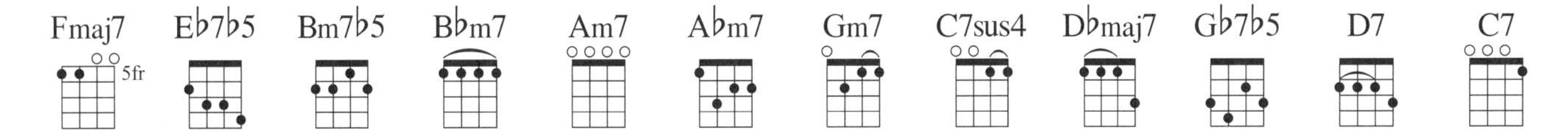

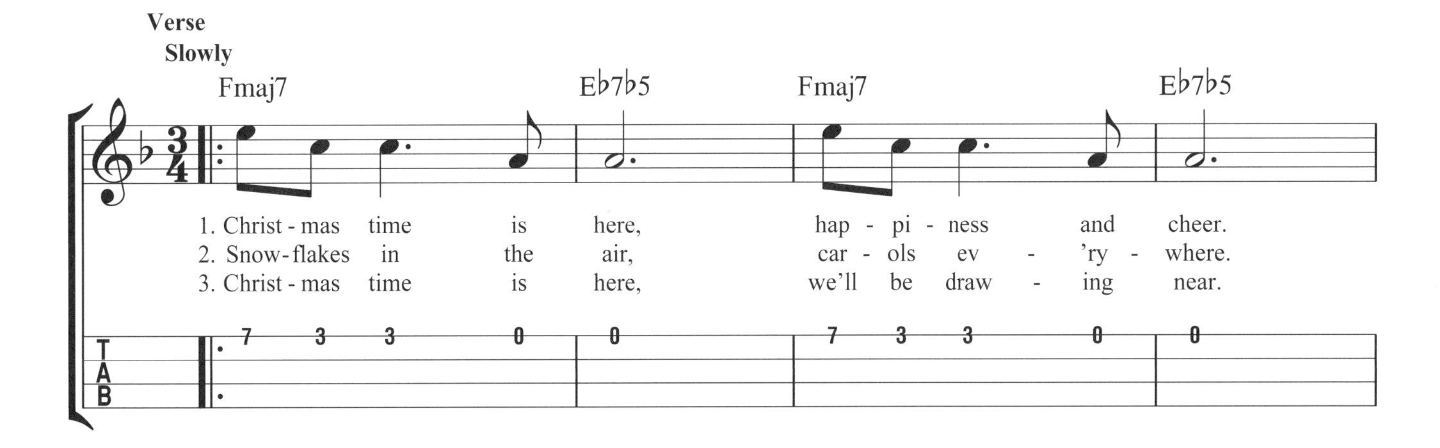

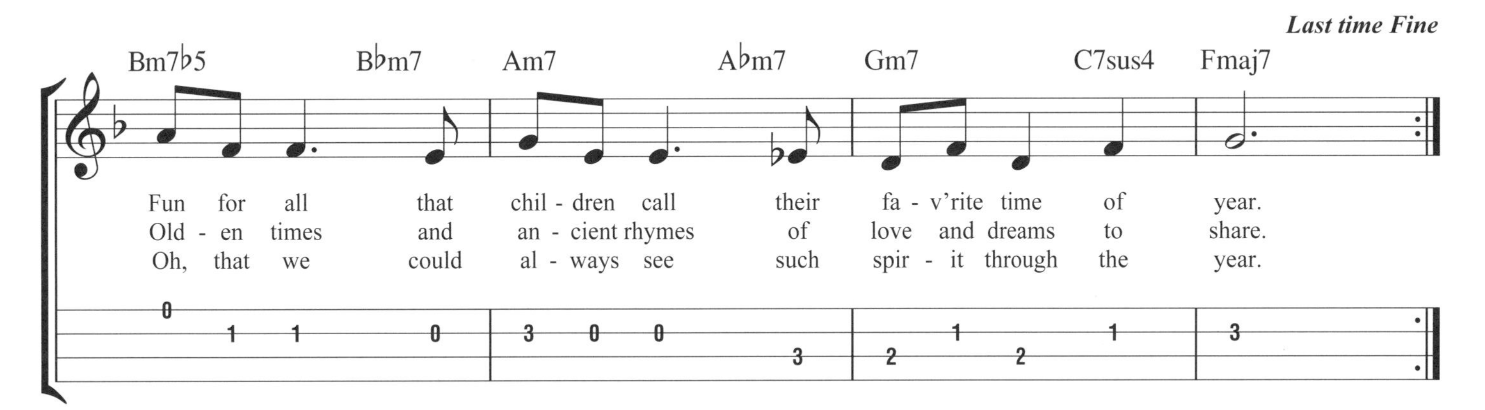

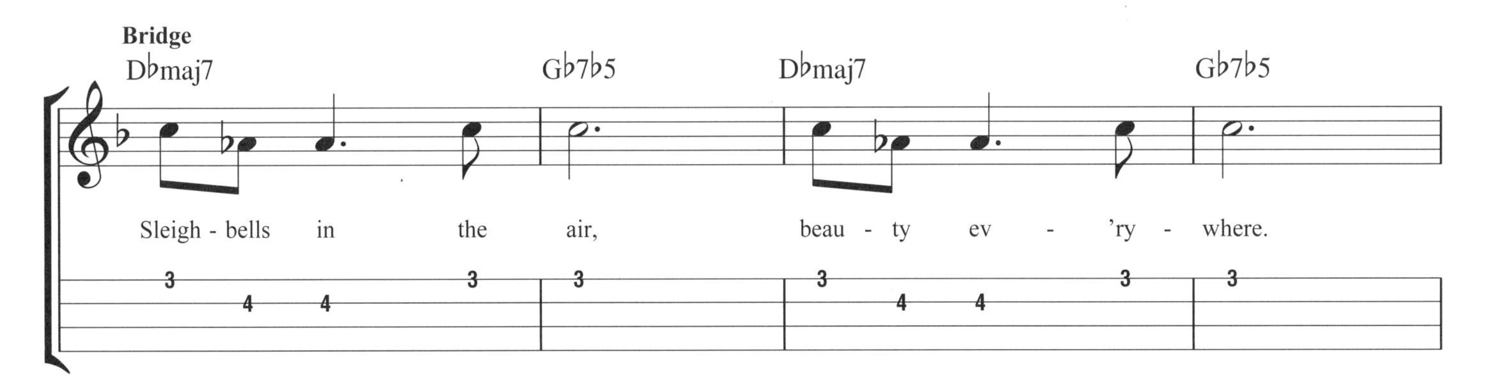

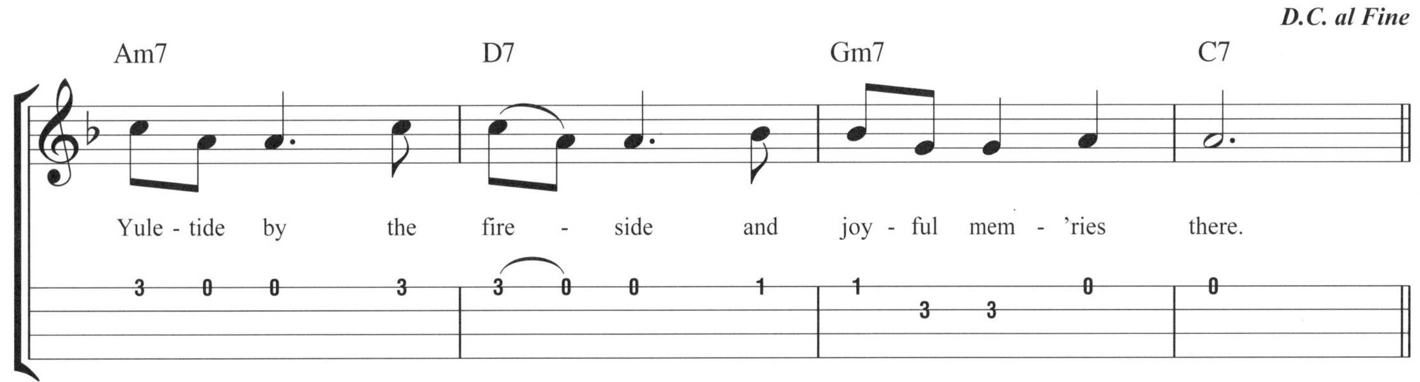

Blue Christmas

Words and Music by Billy Hayes and Jay Johnson

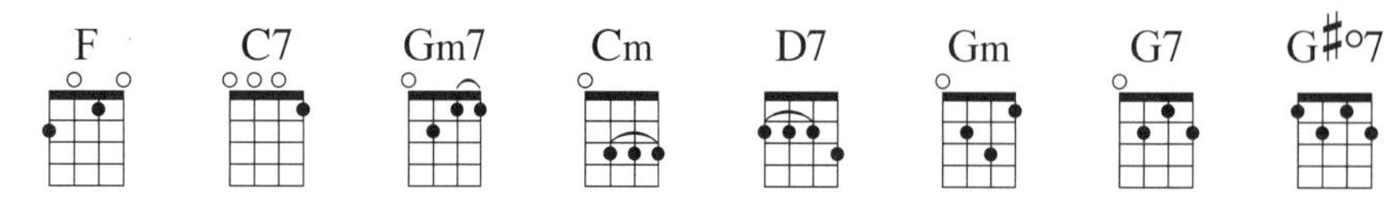

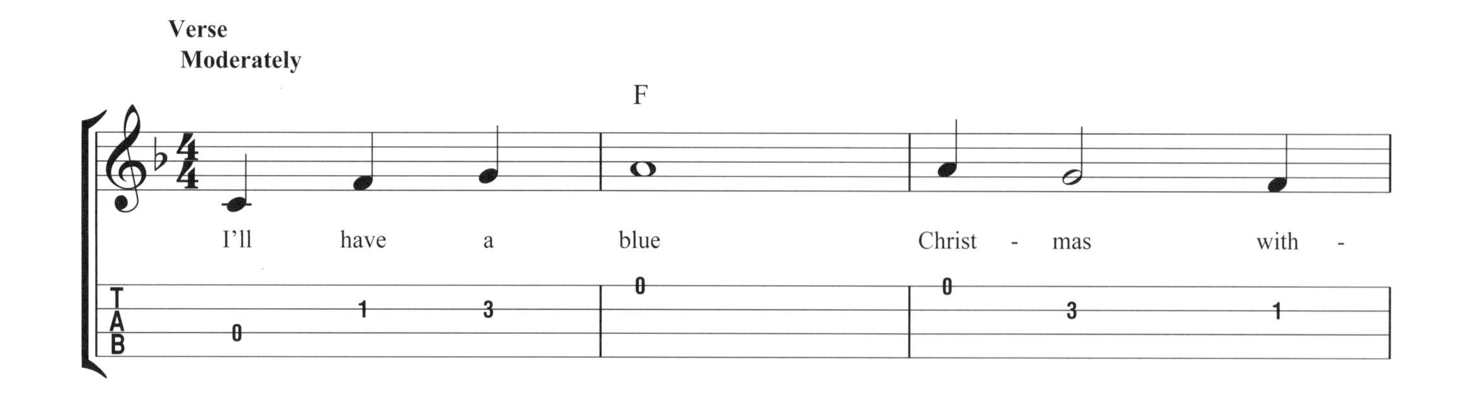

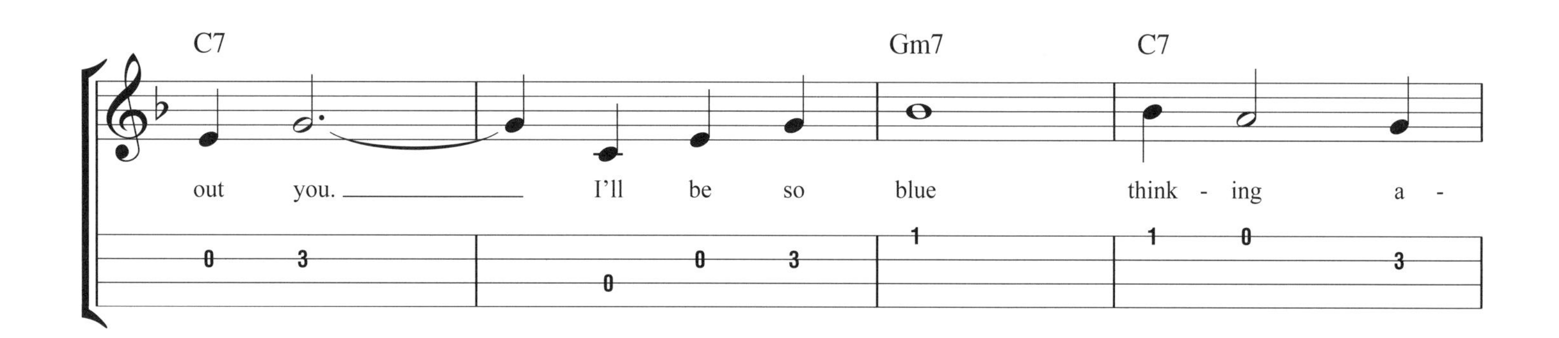

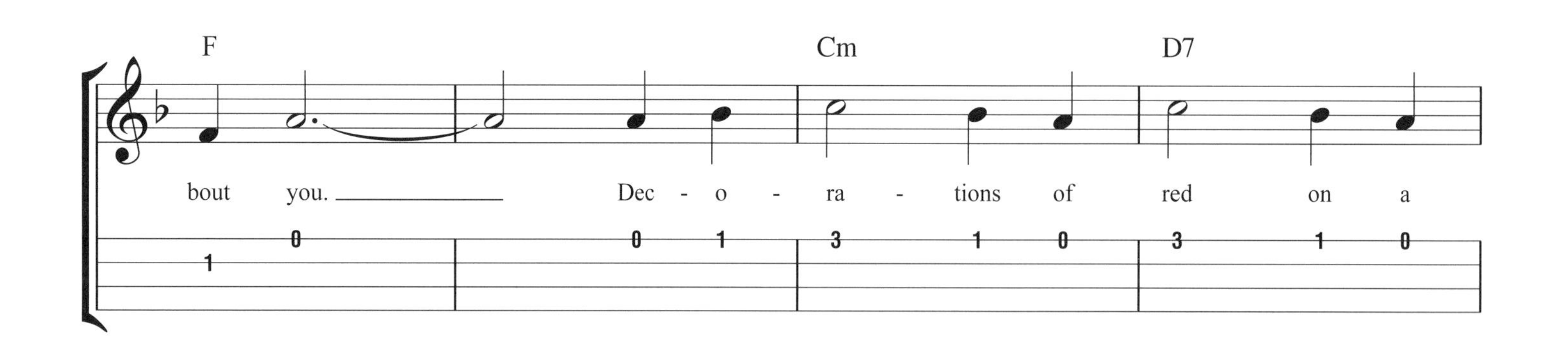

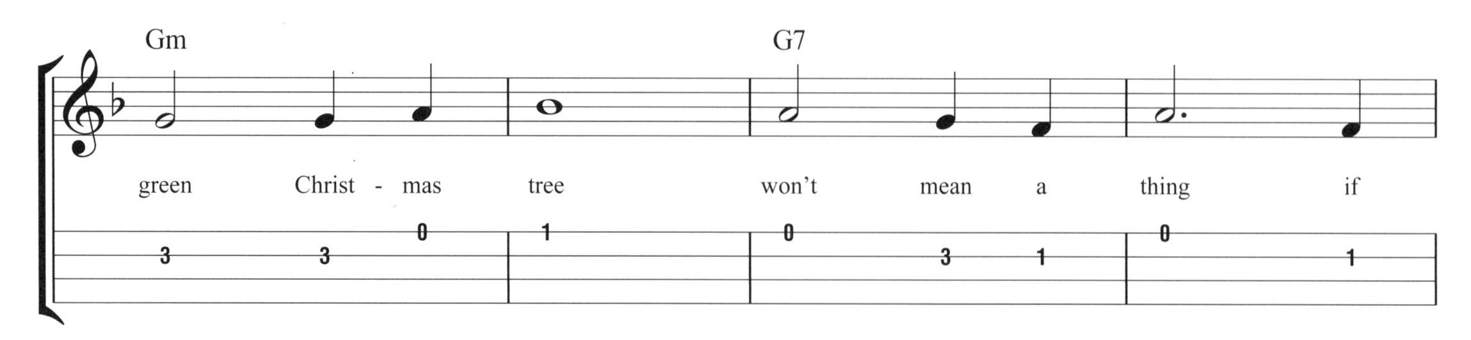

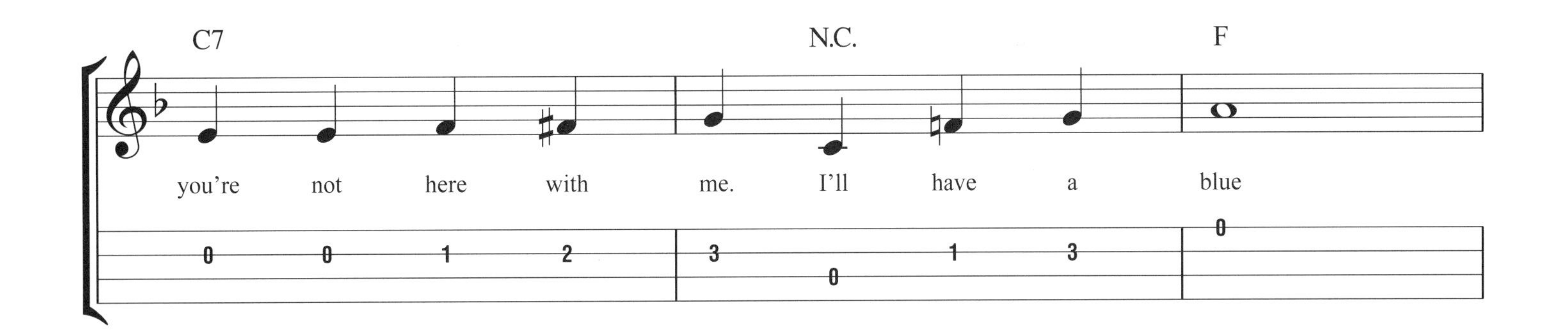
C7 N.C. F
you're not here with me. I'll have a blue

C7 Gm7
Christ - mas; that's cer - tain. And when that blue

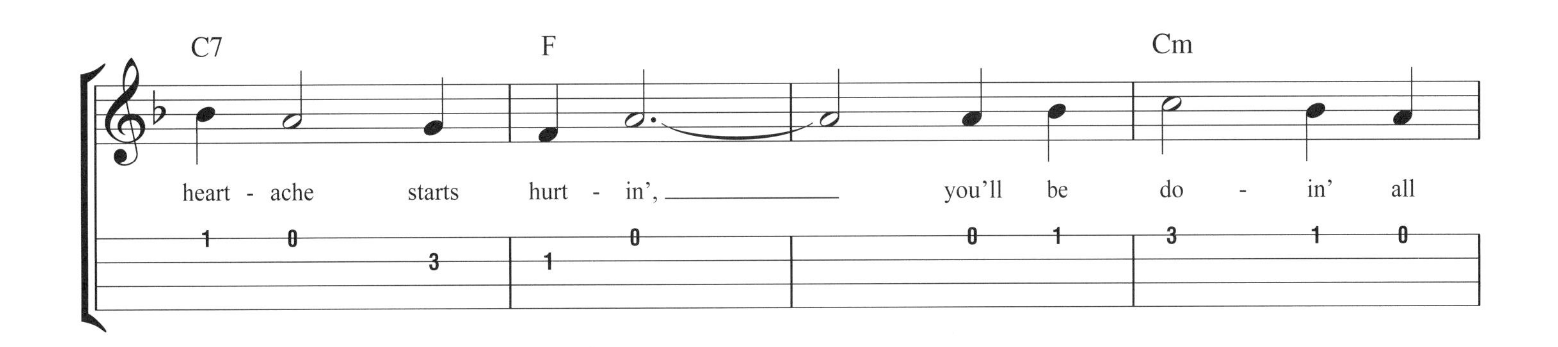
C7 F Cm
heart - ache starts hurt - in', you'll be do - in' all

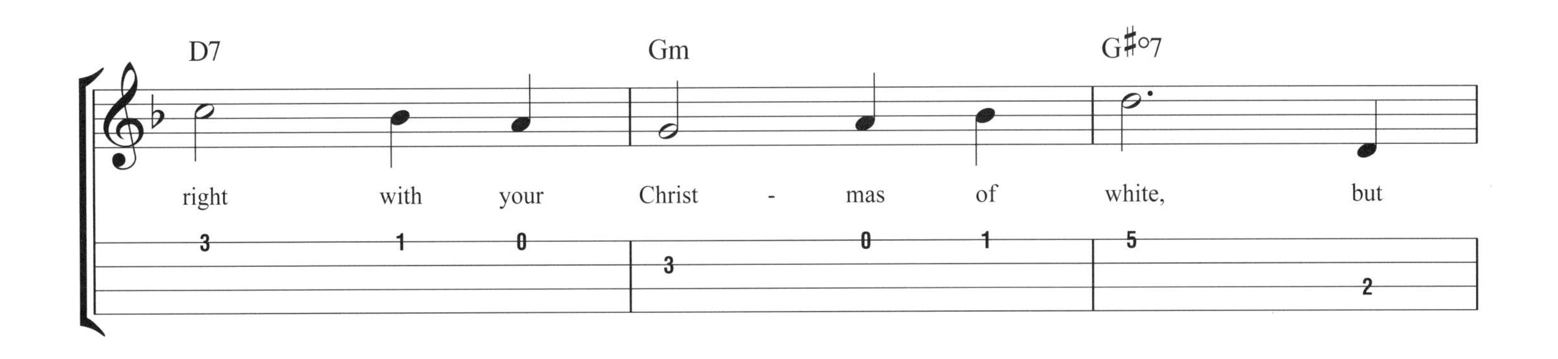
D7 Gm G♯○7
right with your Christ - mas of white, but

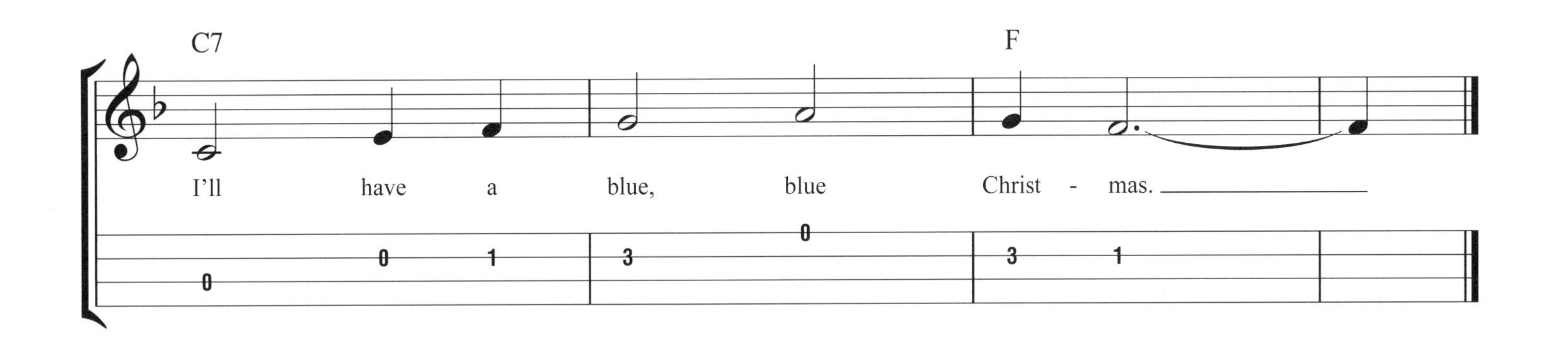
C7 F
I'll have a blue, blue Christ - mas.

The Christmas Song

(Chestnuts Roasting on an Open Fire)

Music and Lyric by Mel Tormé and Robert Wells

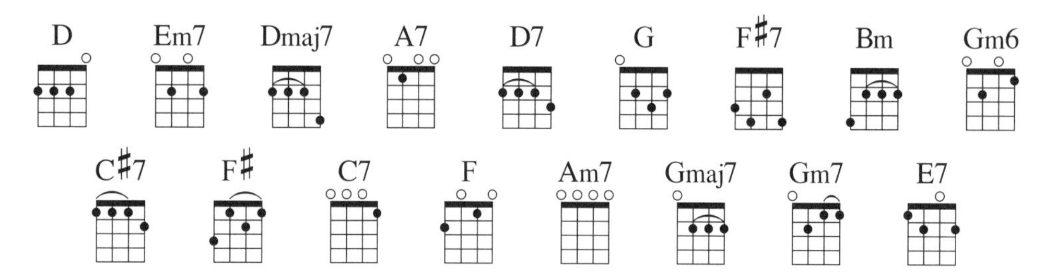

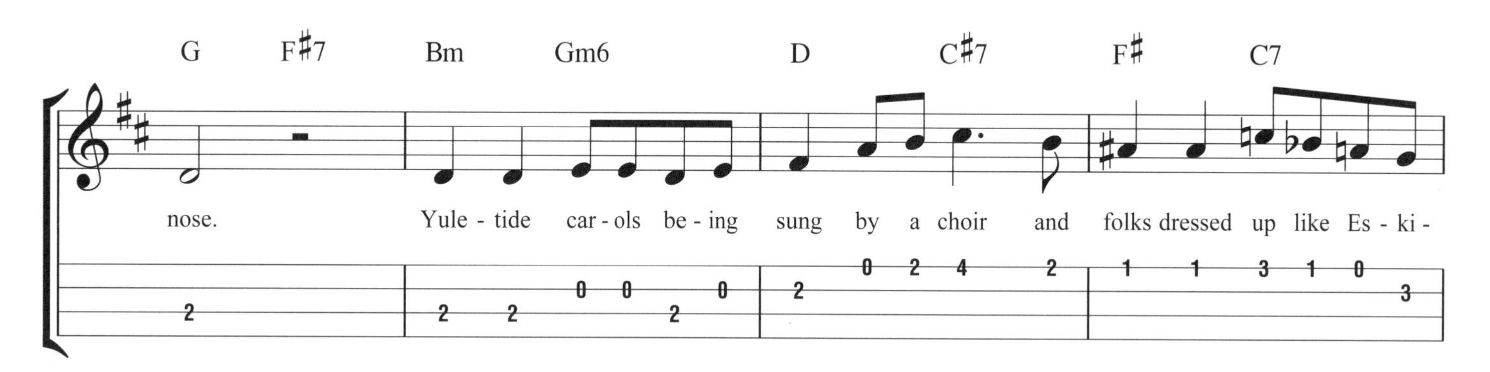

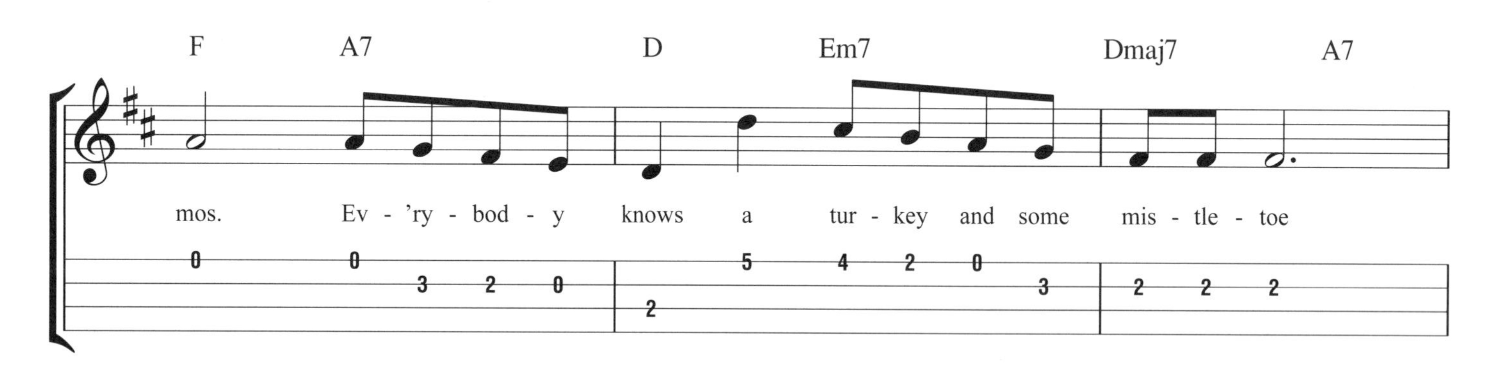

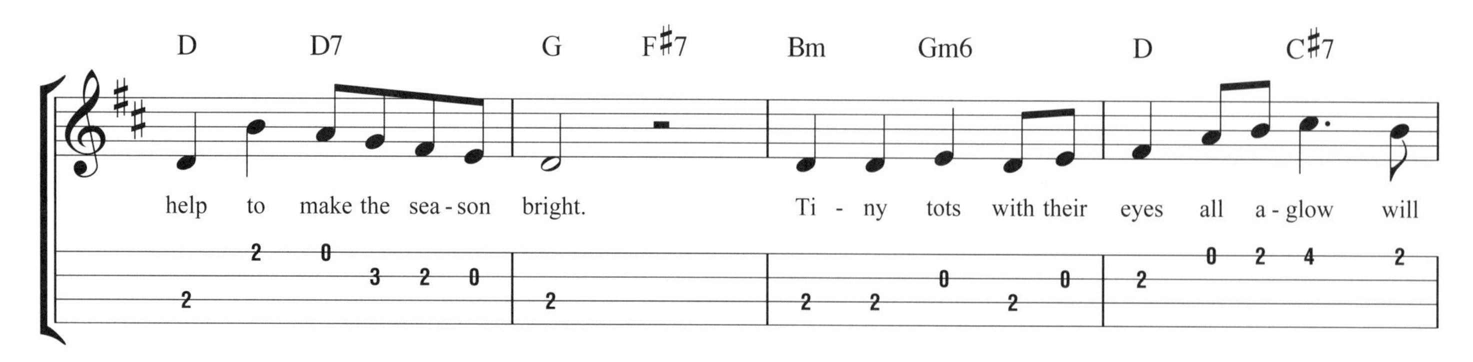

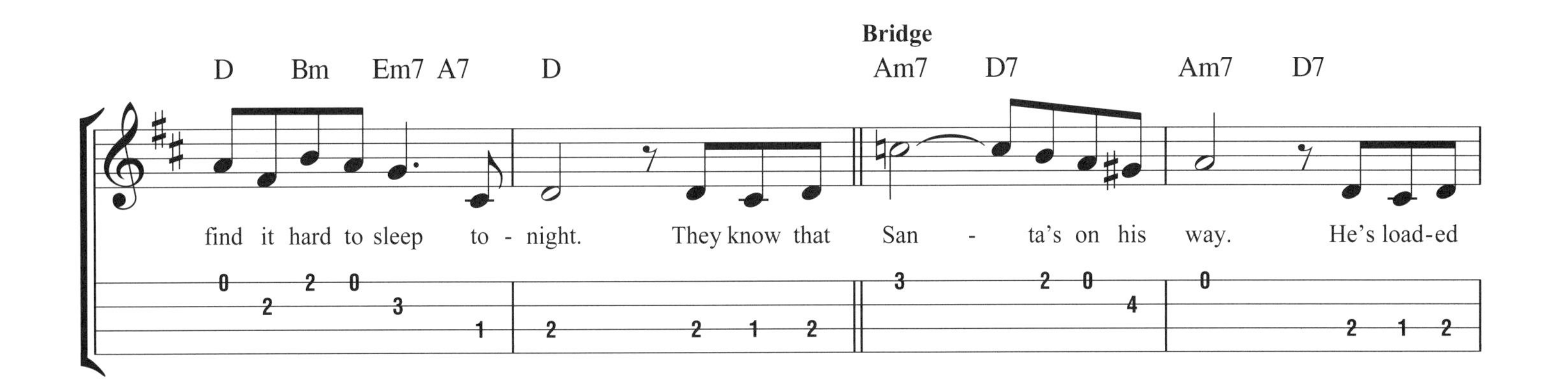
Bridge
D Bm Em7 A7 D Am7 D7 Am7 D7
find it hard to sleep to - night. They know that San - ta's on his way. He's load-ed

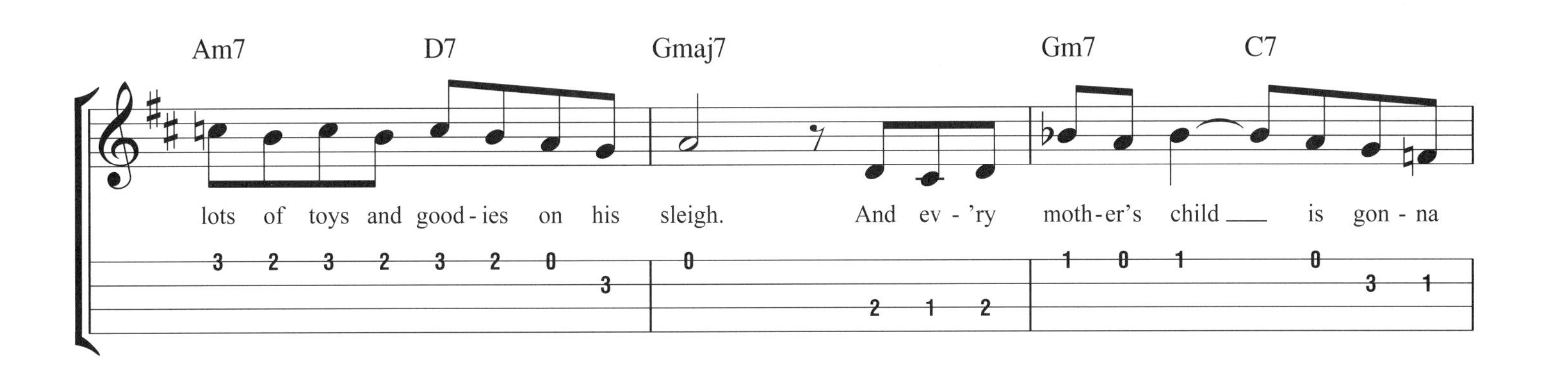
Am7 D7 Gmaj7 Gm7 C7
lots of toys and good - ies on his sleigh. And ev - 'ry moth-er's child is gon - na

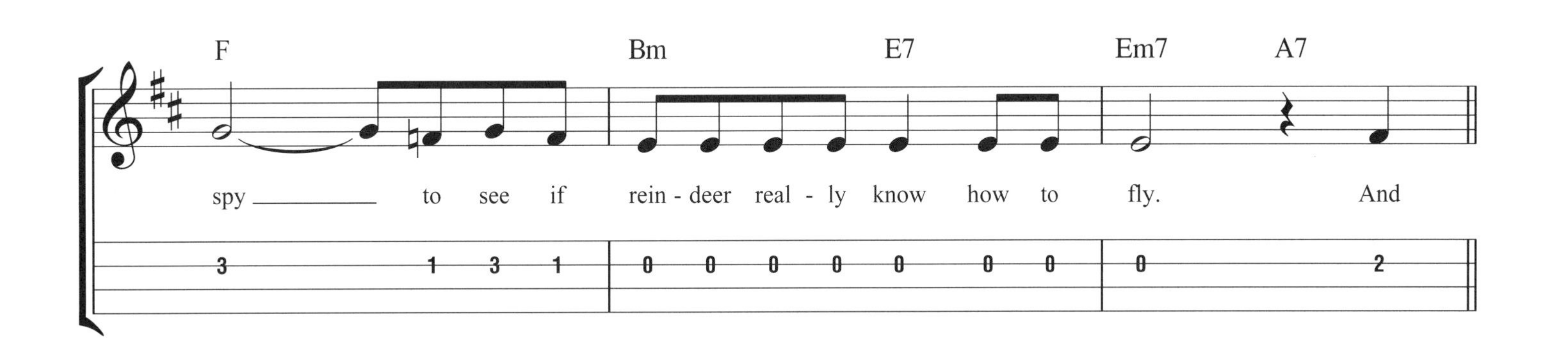
F Bm E7 Em7 A7
spy to see if rein - deer real - ly know how to fly. And

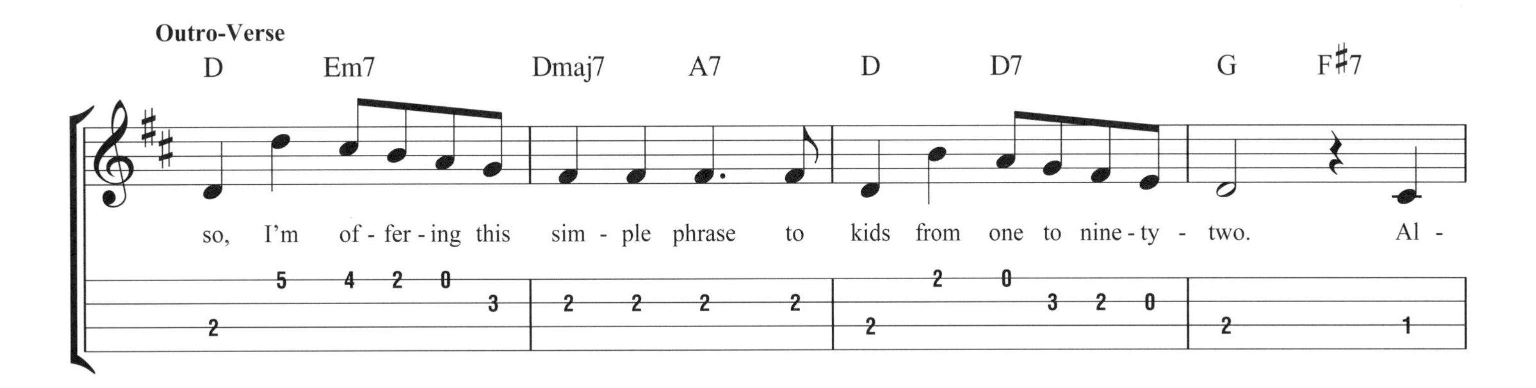
Outro-Verse
D Em7 Dmaj7 A7 D D7 G F♯7
so, I'm of - fer - ing this sim - ple phrase to kids from one to nine - ty - two. Al -

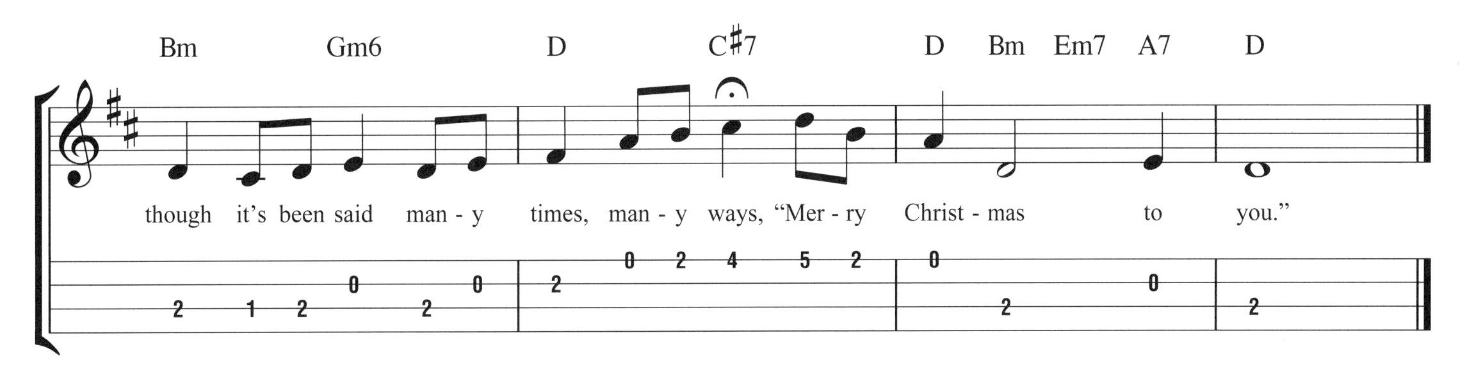
Bm Gm6 D C♯7 D Bm Em7 A7 D
though it's been said man - y times, man - y ways, "Mer - ry Christ - mas to you."

Do You Hear What I Hear

Words and Music by Noel Regney and Gloria Shayne

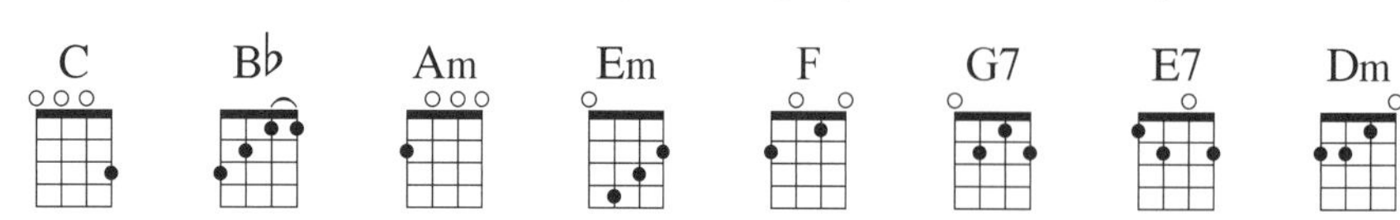

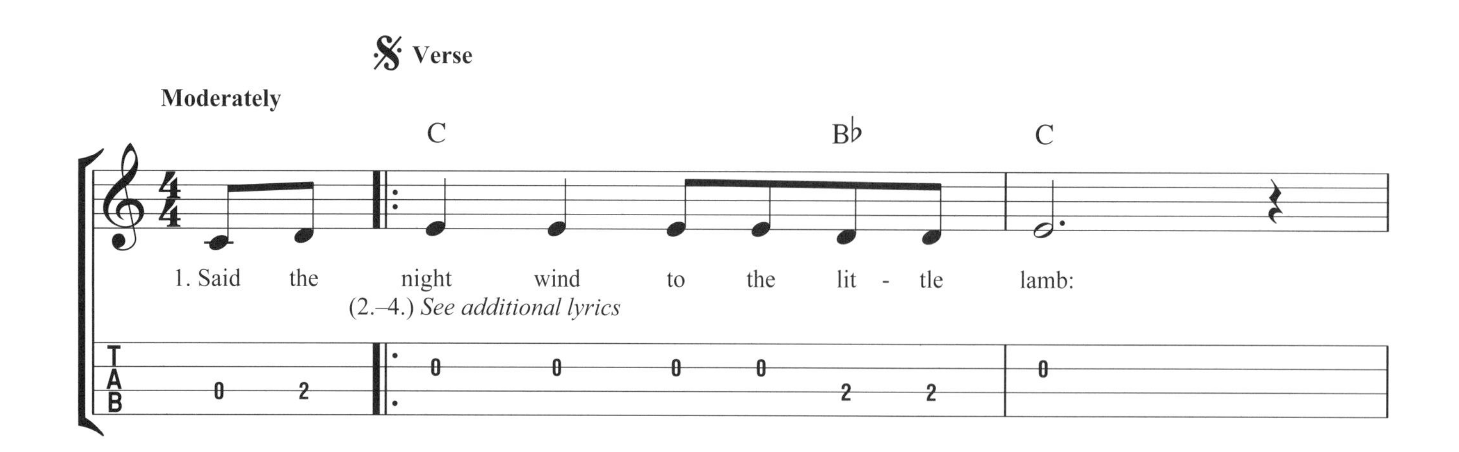

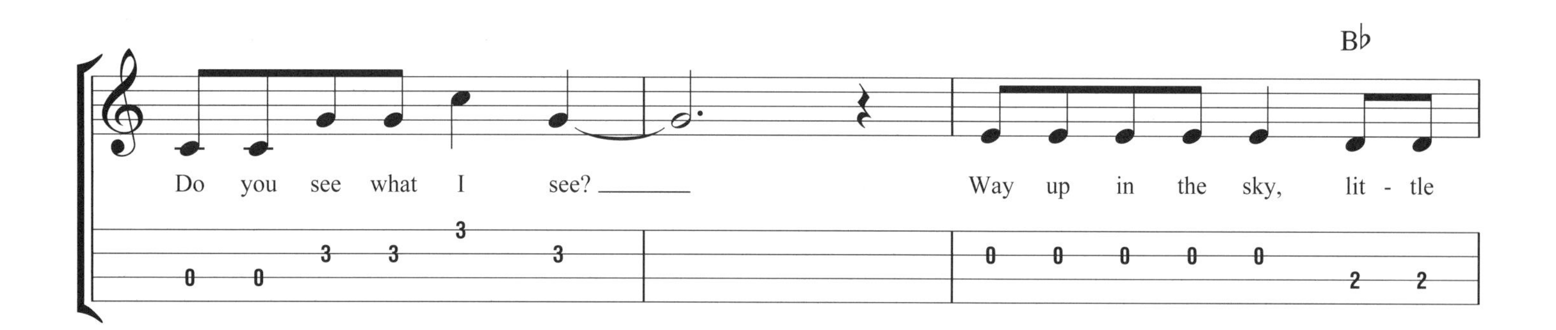

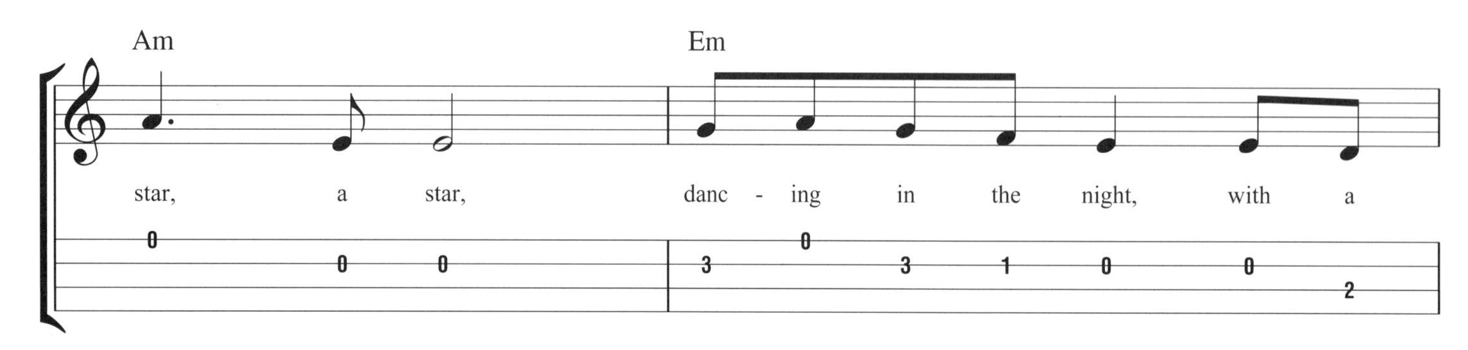

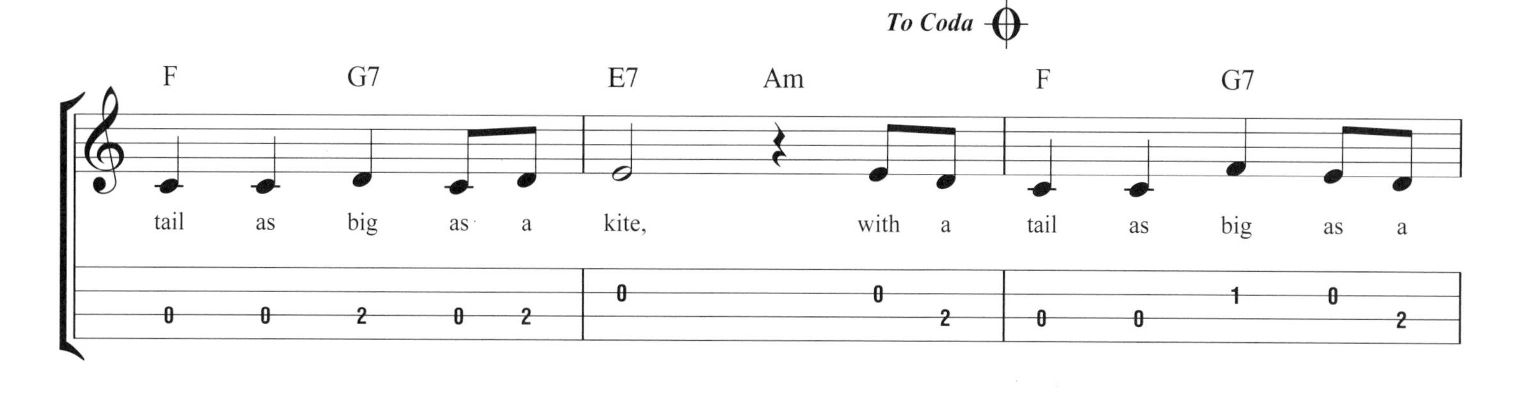

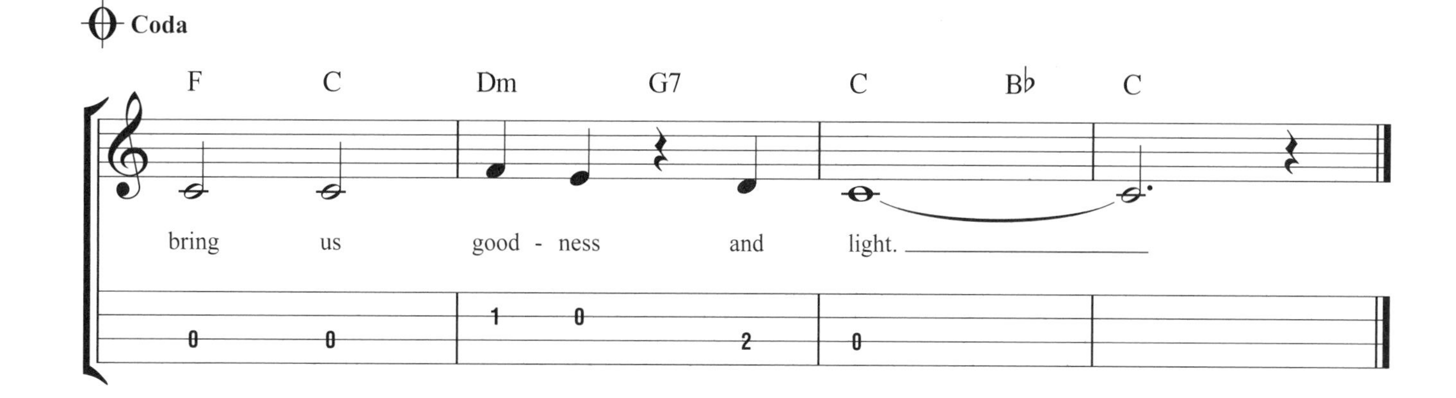

Additional Lyrics

2. Said the little lamb to the shepherd boy:
   Do you hear what I hear?
   Ringing through the sky, shepherd boy,
   Do you hear what I hear?
   A song, a song, high above the tree,
   With a voice as big as the sea,
   With a voice as big as the sea.

3. Said the shepherd boy to the mighty king:
   Do you know what I know?
   In your palace warm, mighty king,
   Do you know what I know?
   A Child, a Child shivers in the cold;
   Let us bring Him silver and gold,
   Let us bring Him silver and gold.

4. Said the king to the people ev'rywhere:
   Listen to what I say!
   Pray for peace, people ev'rywhere.
   Listen to what I say!
   The Child, the Child, sleeping in the night,
   He will bring us goodness and light,
   He will bring us goodness and light.

Feliz Navidad

Music and Lyrics by José Feliciano

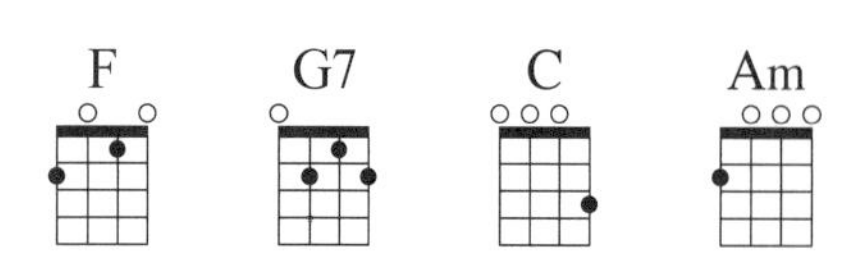

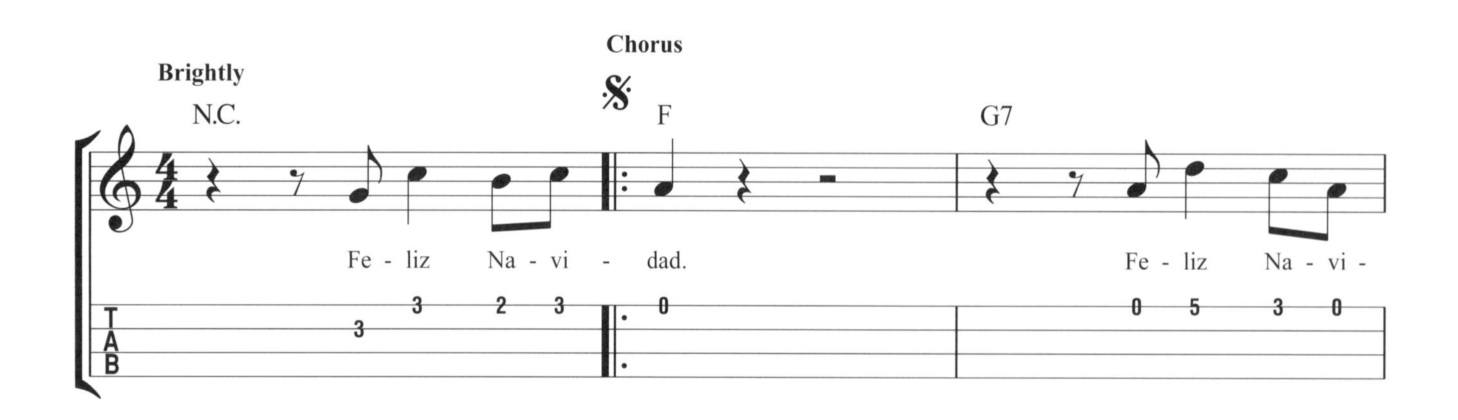

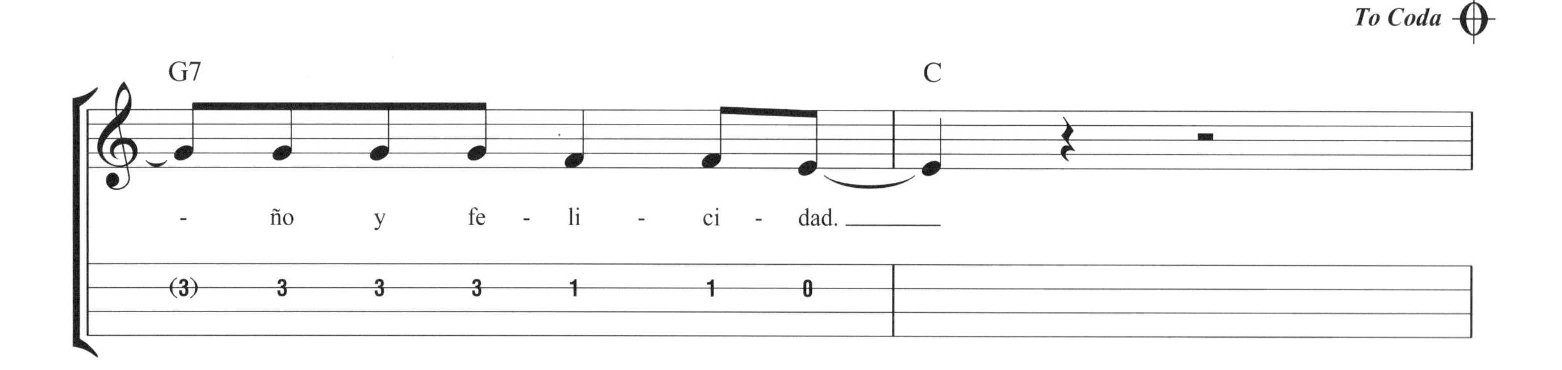

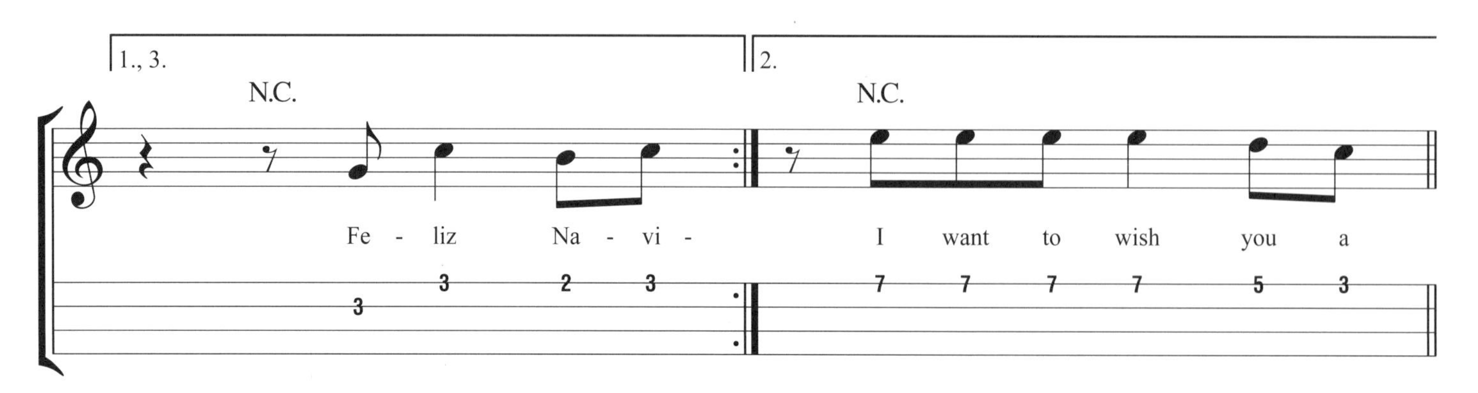

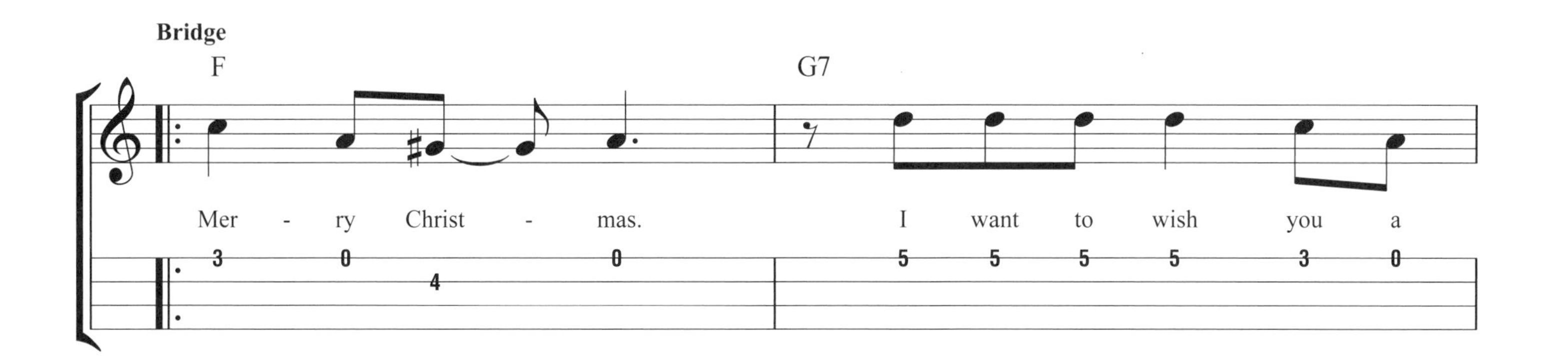
Bridge
F
G7
Mer - ry Christ - mas.
I want to wish you a
3 0 4 0
5 5 5 5 3 0

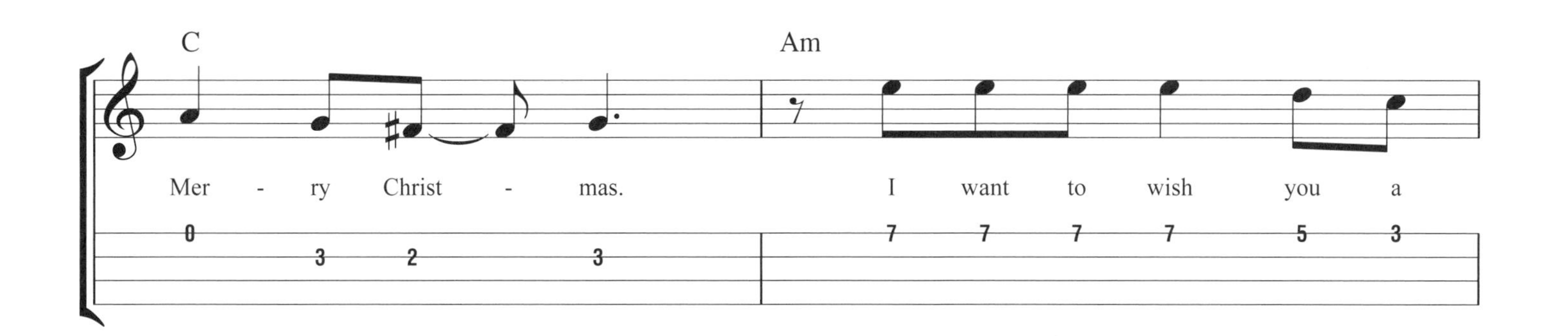
C
Am
Mer - ry Christ - mas.
I want to wish you a
0 3 2 3
7 7 7 7 5 3

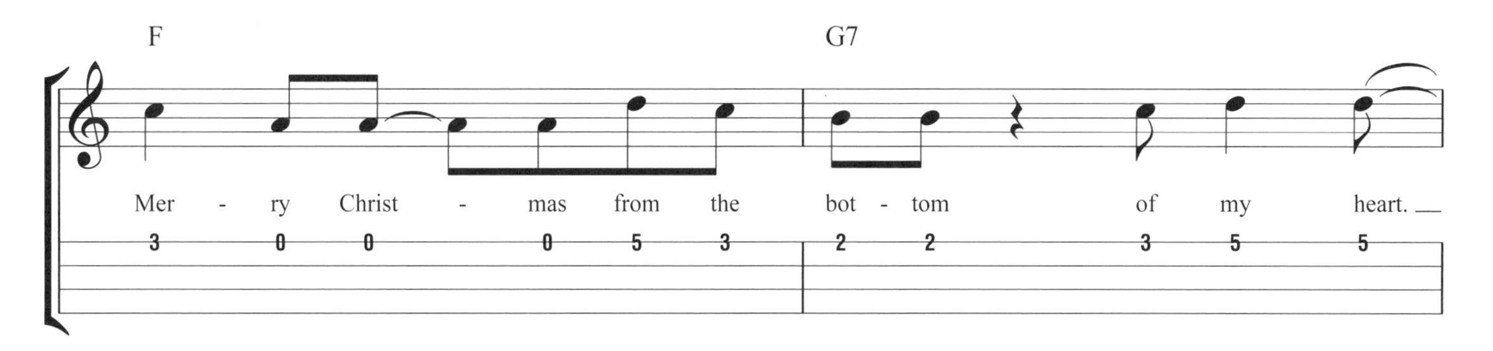
F
G7
Mer - ry Christ - mas from the
bot - tom of my heart.
3 0 0 0 5 3
2 2 3 5 5

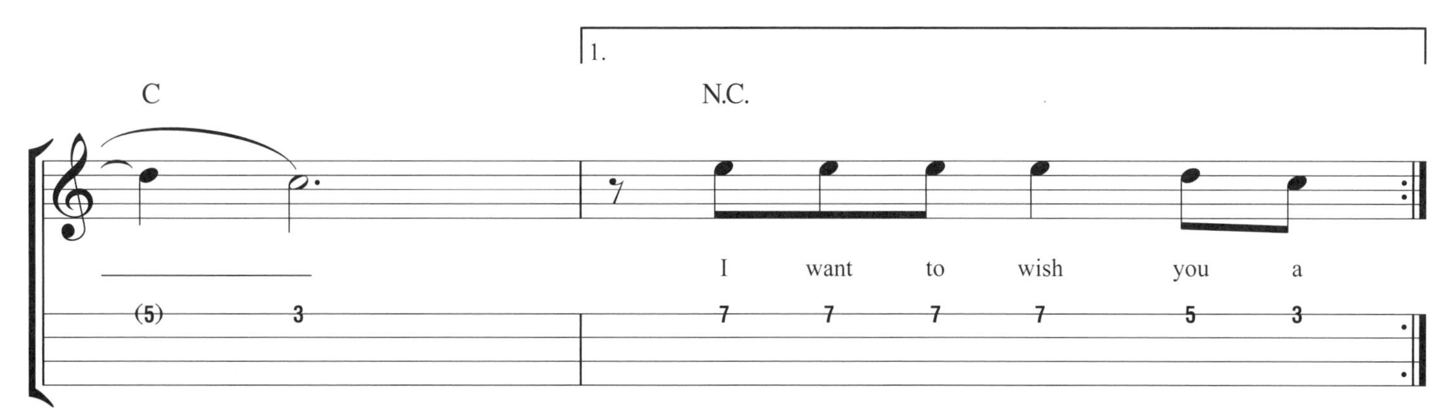
1.
C
N.C.
I want to wish you a
(5) 3
7 7 7 7 5 3

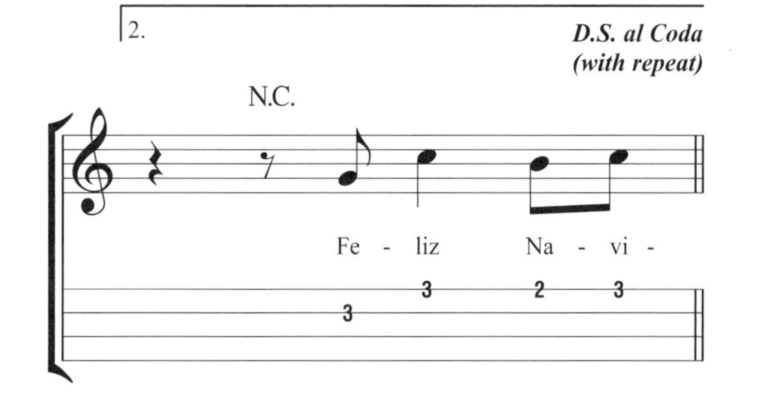
2.
D.S. al Coda
(with repeat)
N.C.
Fe - liz Na - vi -
3 3 2 3

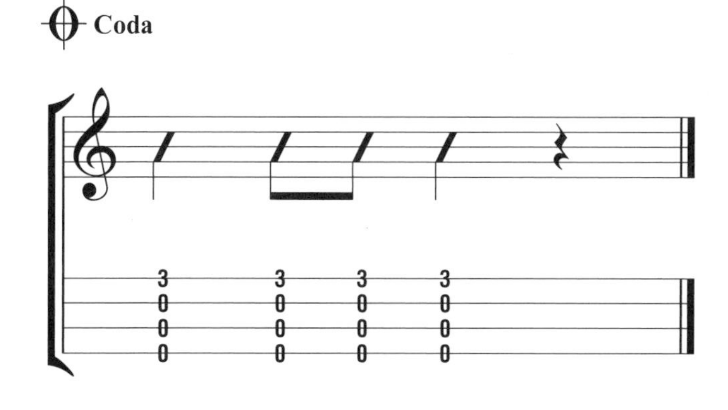
Coda

Frosty the Snow Man

Words and Music by Steve Nelson and Jack Rollins

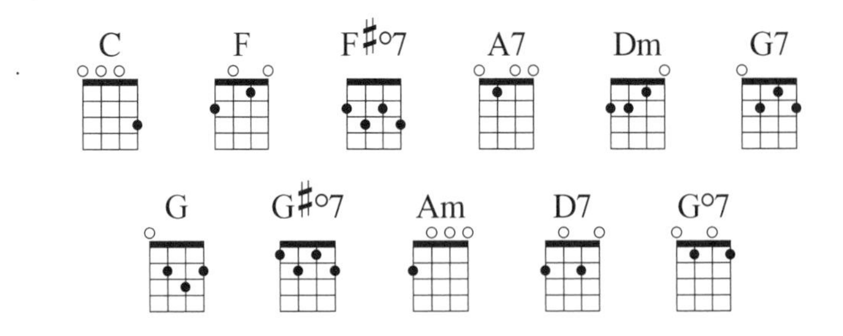

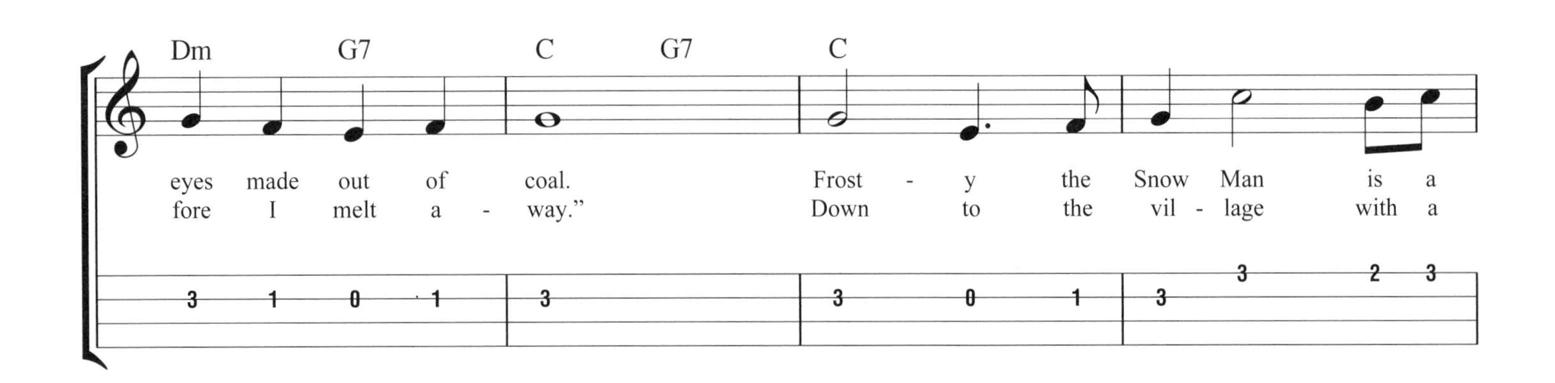

F C F F♯°7
fair - y tale, they say. He was made of snow, but the
broom - stick in his hand, run - ning here and there, all a -

C A7 Dm G7 C C7
chil - dren know how he came to life one day. There
round the square, say - in', "Catch me if you can." He

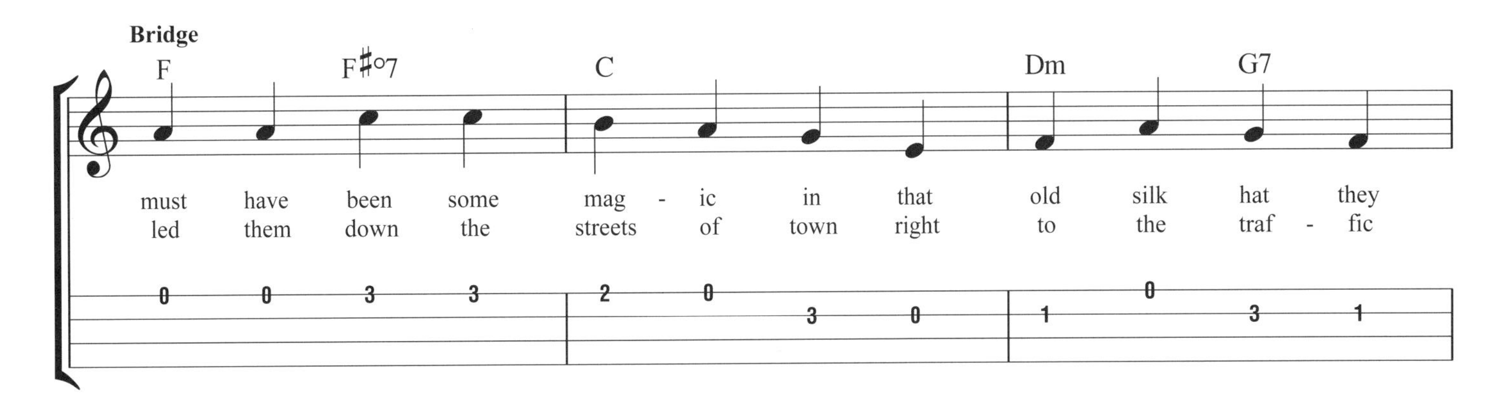
Bridge
F F♯°7 C Dm G7
must have been some mag - ic in that old silk hat they
led them down the streets of town right to the traf - fic

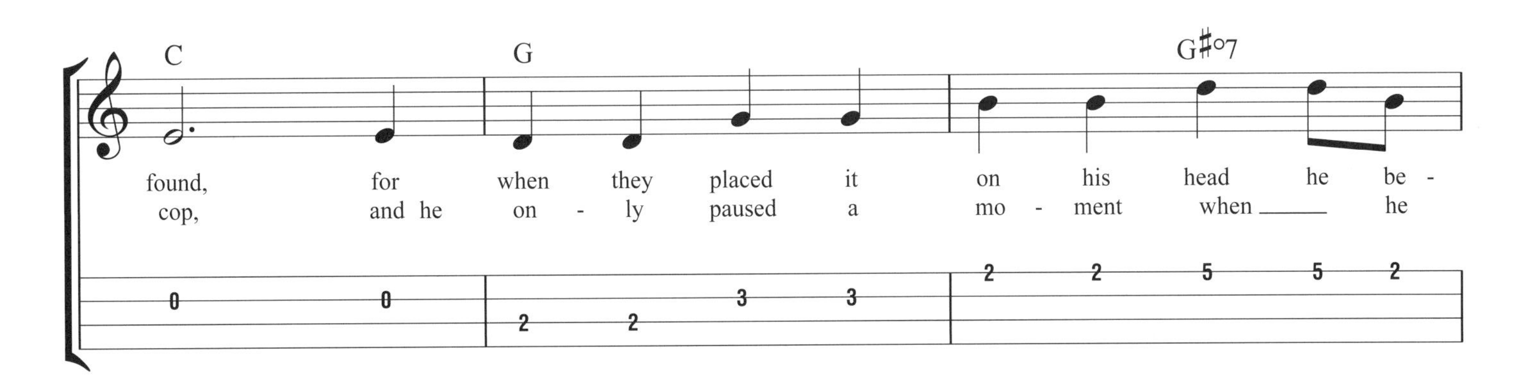
C G G♯°7
found, for when they placed it on his head he be -
cop, and he on - ly paused a mo - ment when he

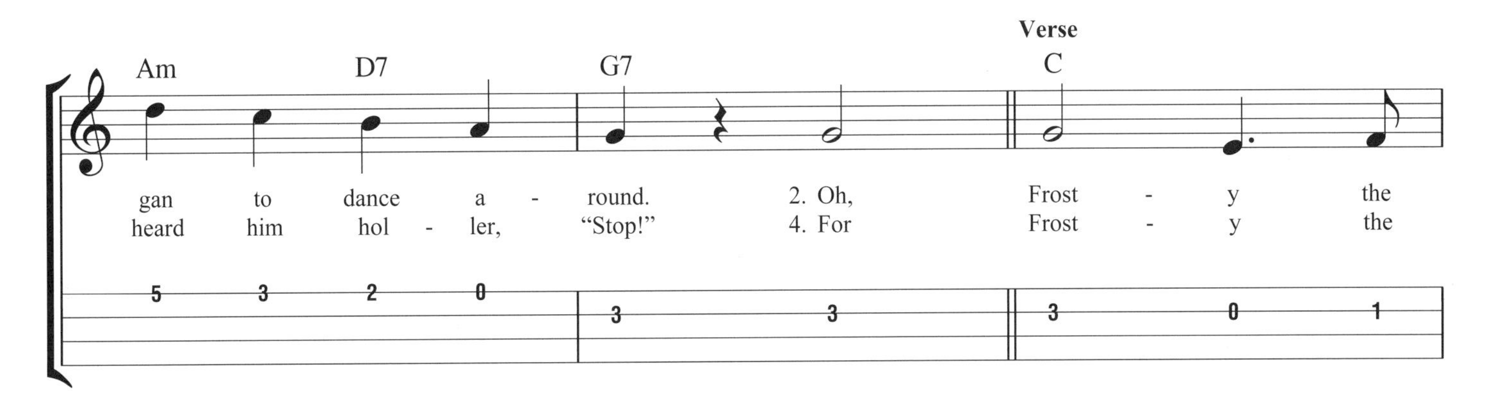
Verse
Am D7 G7 C
gan to dance a - round. 2. Oh, Frost - y the
heard him hol - ler, "Stop!" 4. For Frost - y the

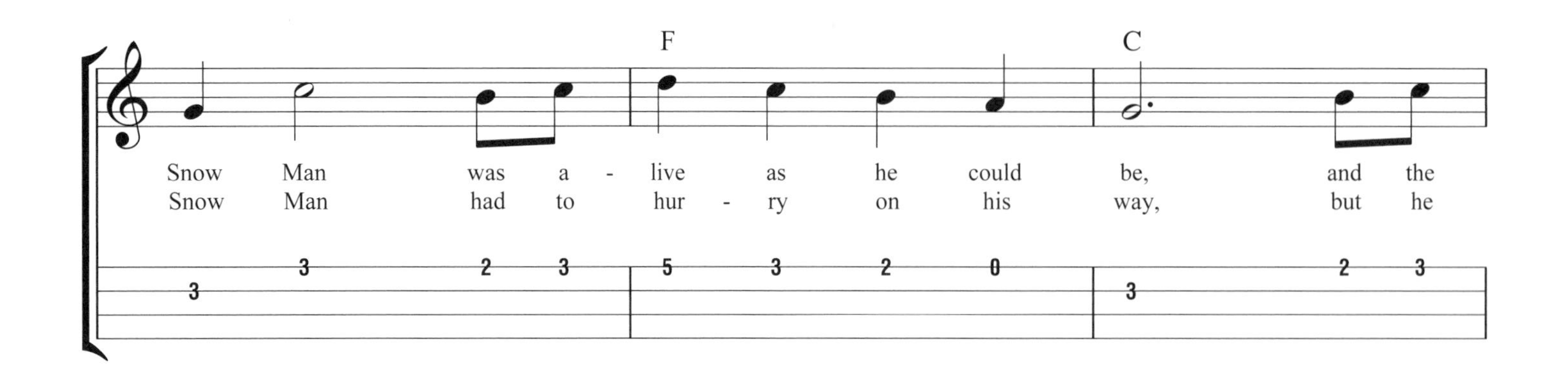
F
C
Snow Man was a - live as he could be, and the
Snow Man had to hur - ry on his way, but he

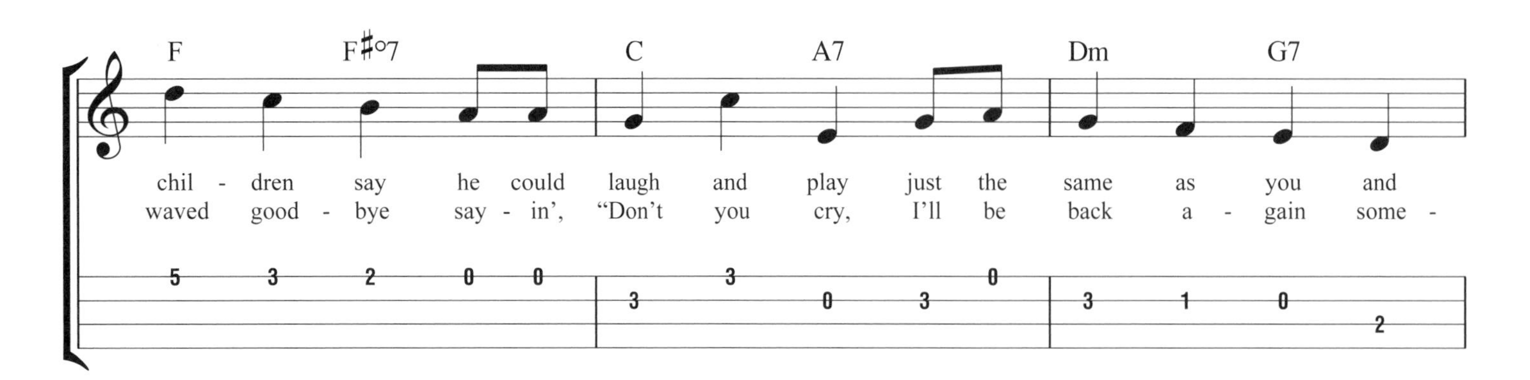
F
F♯°7
C
A7
Dm
G7
chil - dren say he could laugh and play just the same as you and
waved good - bye say - in', "Don't you cry, I'll be back a - gain some -

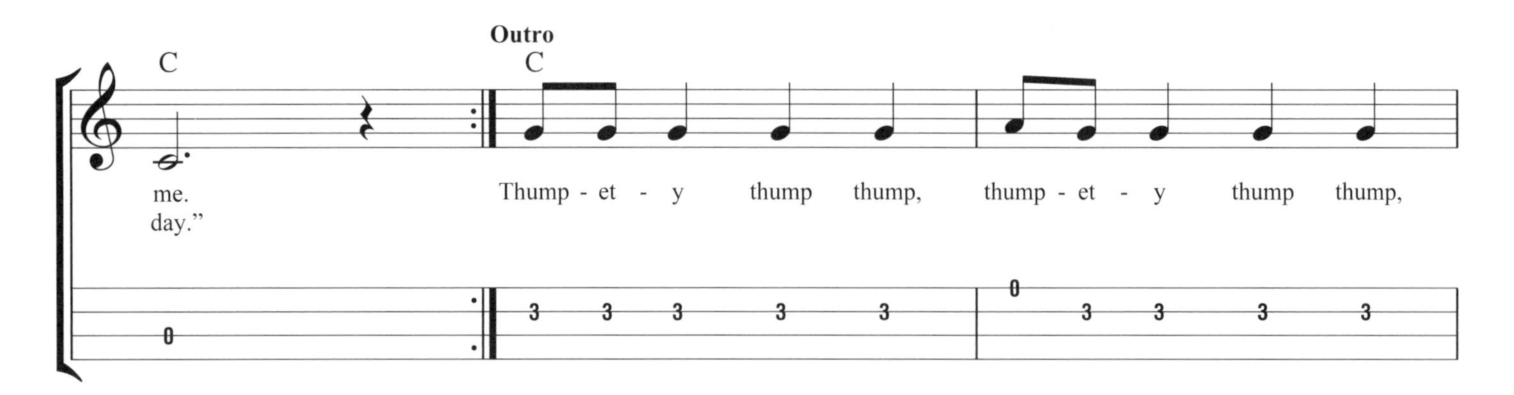
C
Outro
C
me.
day."
Thump - et - y thump thump, thump - et - y thump thump,

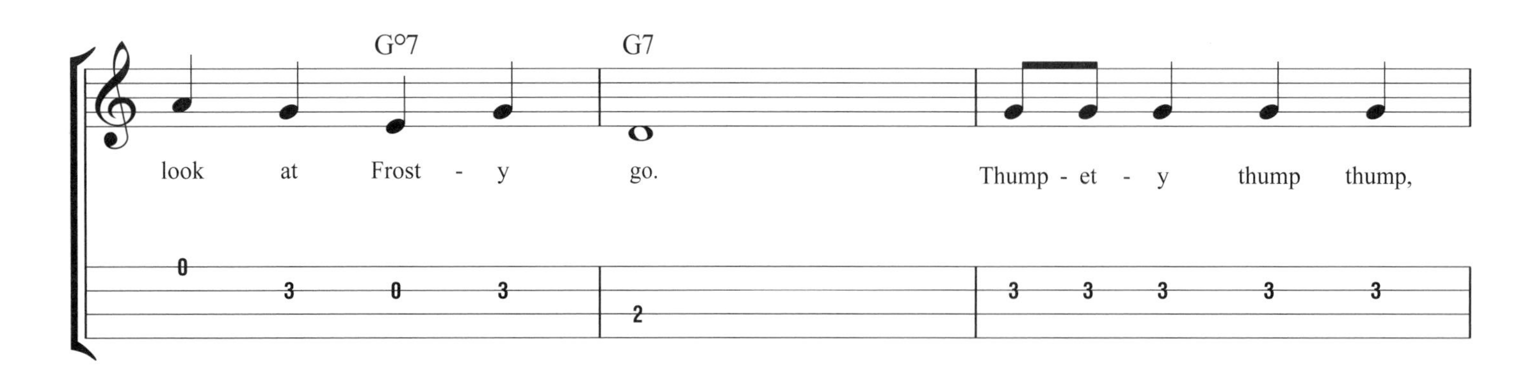
G°7
G7
look at Frost - y go.
Thump - et - y thump thump,

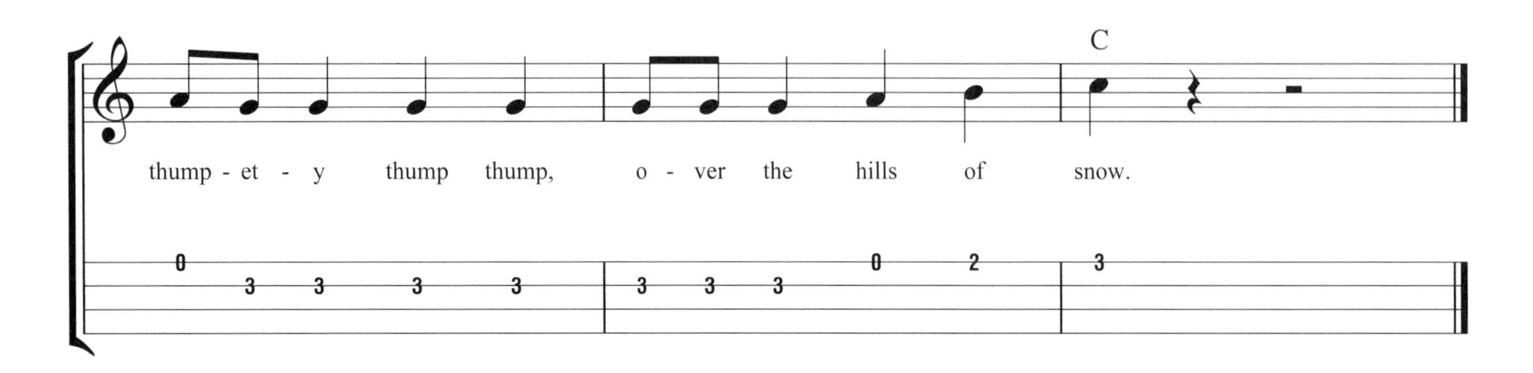
C
thump - et - y thump thump, o - ver the hills of snow.

(There's No Place Like)

Home for the Holidays

Words and Music by Al Stillman and Robert Allen

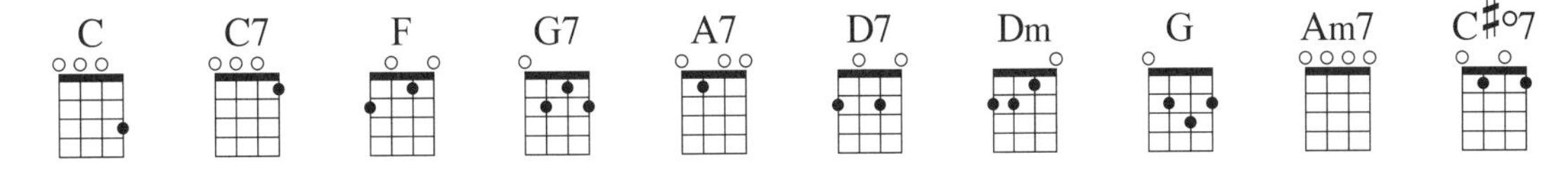

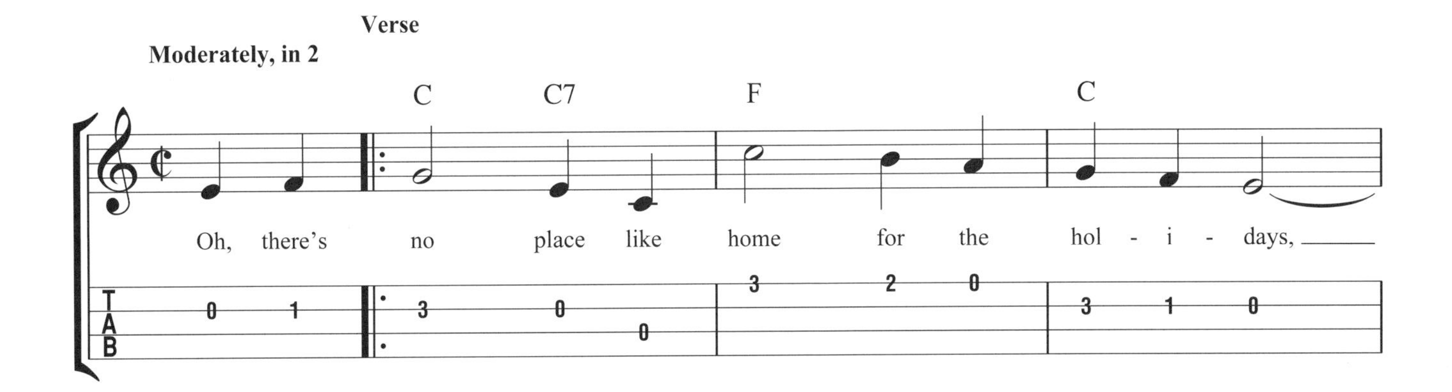

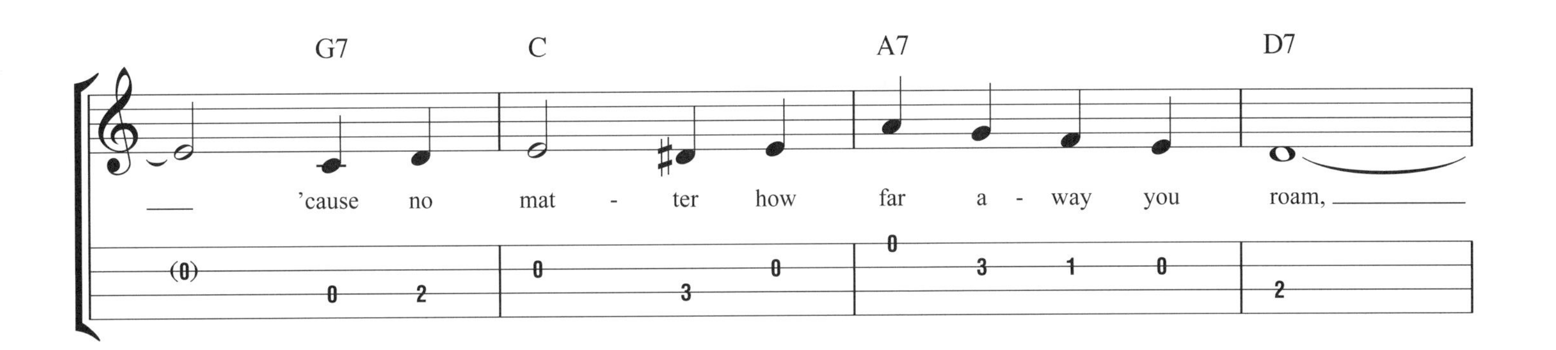

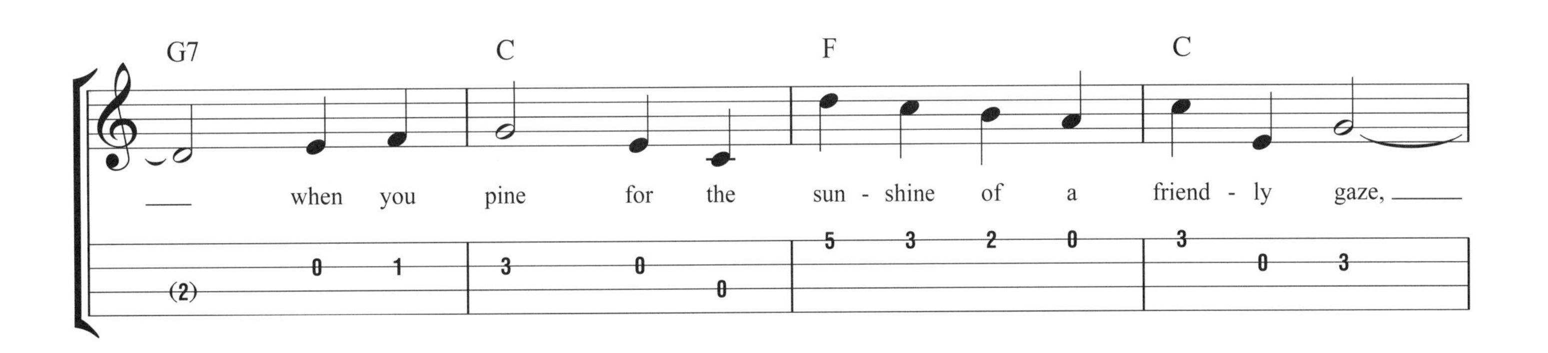

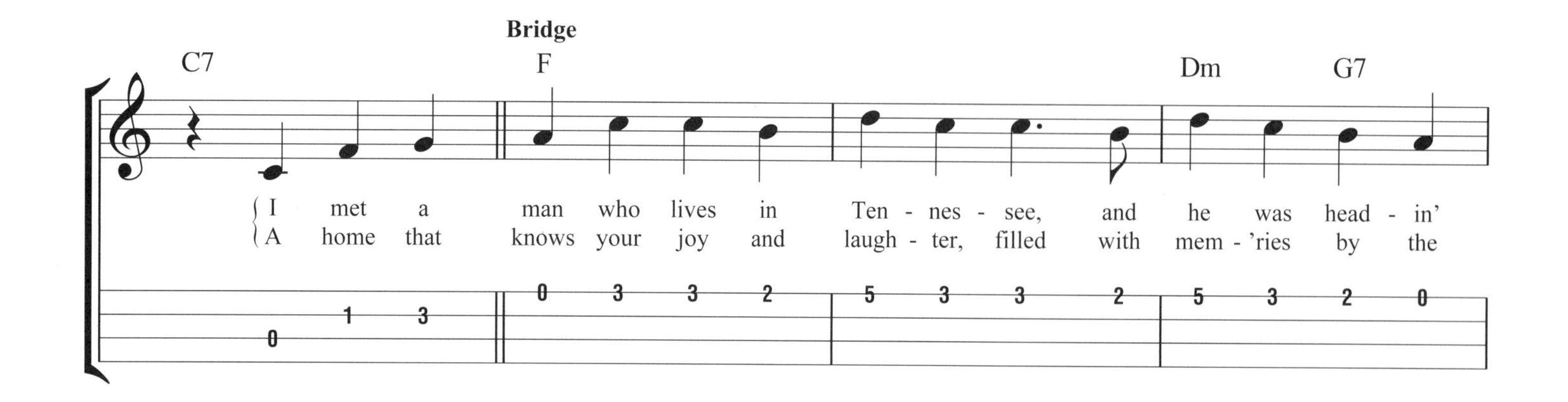
Bridge
C7 F Dm G7
I met a man who lives in Ten - nes - see, and he was head - in'
A home that knows your joy and laugh - ter, filled with mem - 'ries by the

C G7 Dm G7 C
for Penn - syl - va - nia and some home - made pump - kin pie.
score, is a home you're glad to wel - come with your heart.

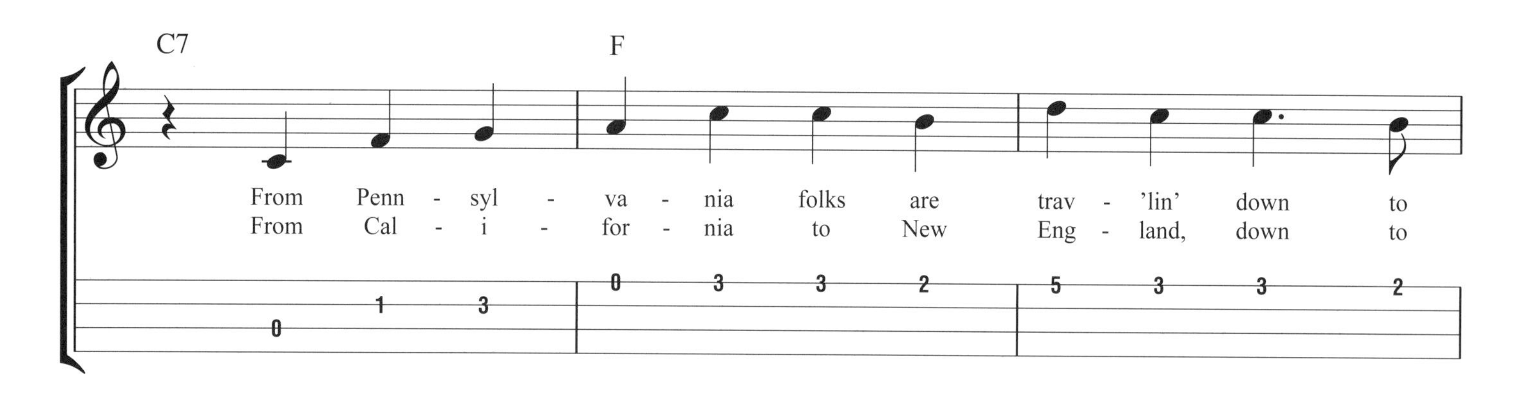
C7 F
From Penn - syl - va - nia folks are trav - 'lin' down to
From Cal - i - for - nia to New Eng - land, down to

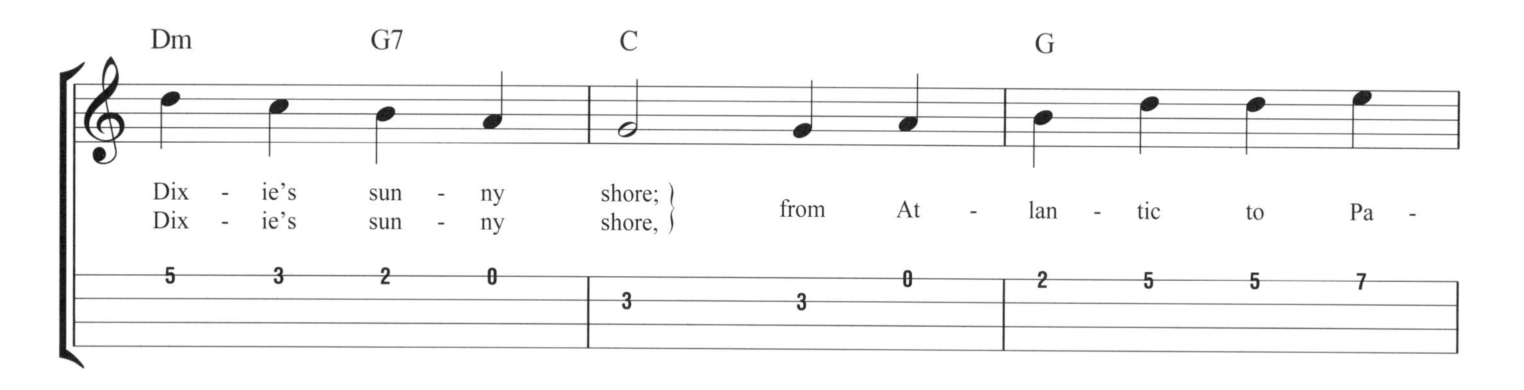
Dm G7 C G
Dix - ie's sun - ny shore;
Dix - ie's sun - ny shore,
from At - lan - tic to Pa -

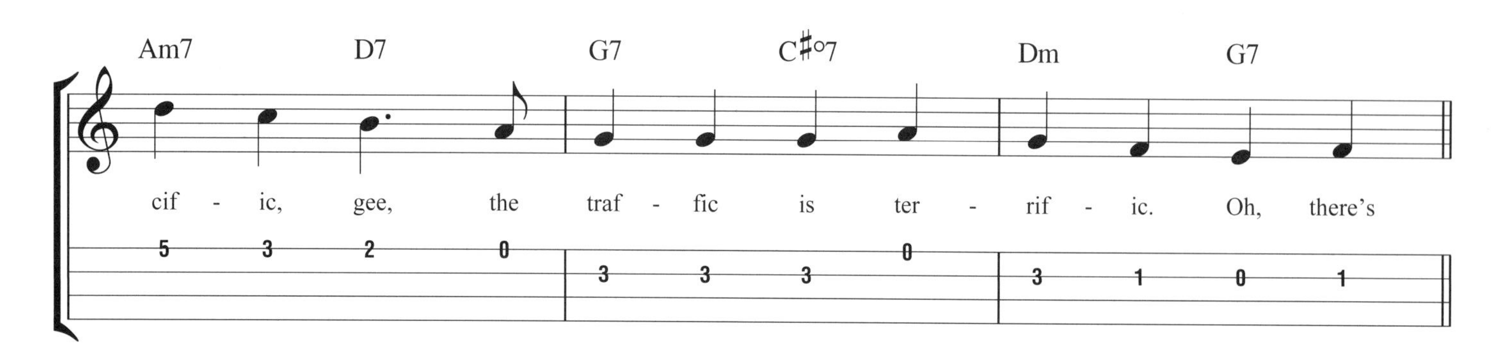
Am7 D7 G7 C♯°7 Dm G7
cif - ic, gee, the traf - fic is ter - rif - ic. Oh, there's

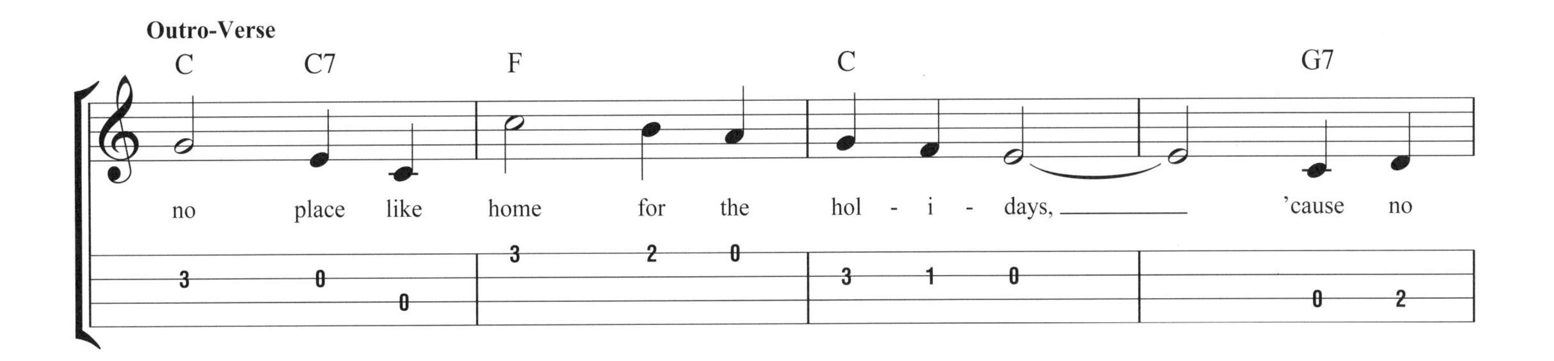
Outro-Verse
C C7 F C G7
no place like home for the hol - i - days, 'cause no
3 0 0 3 2 0 3 1 0 0 2

C A7 D7 G7
mat - ter how far a - way you roam, if you
0 3 0 0 3 1 0 2 0 1

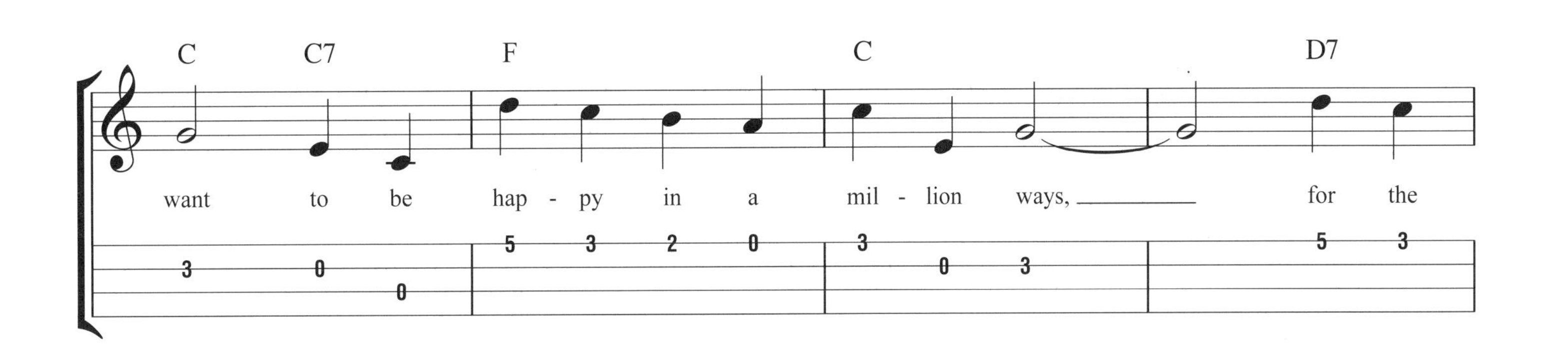
C C7 F C D7
want to be hap - py in a mil - lion ways, for the
3 0 0 5 3 2 0 3 0 3 5 3

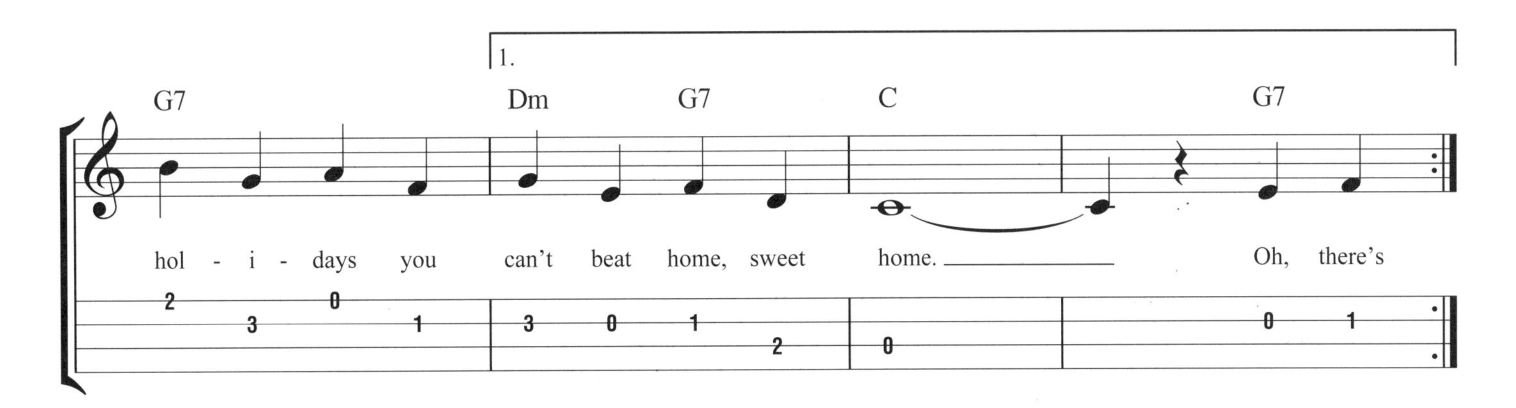
1.
G7 Dm G7 C G7
hol - i - days you can't beat home, sweet home. Oh, there's
2 3 0 1 3 0 1 2 0 0 1

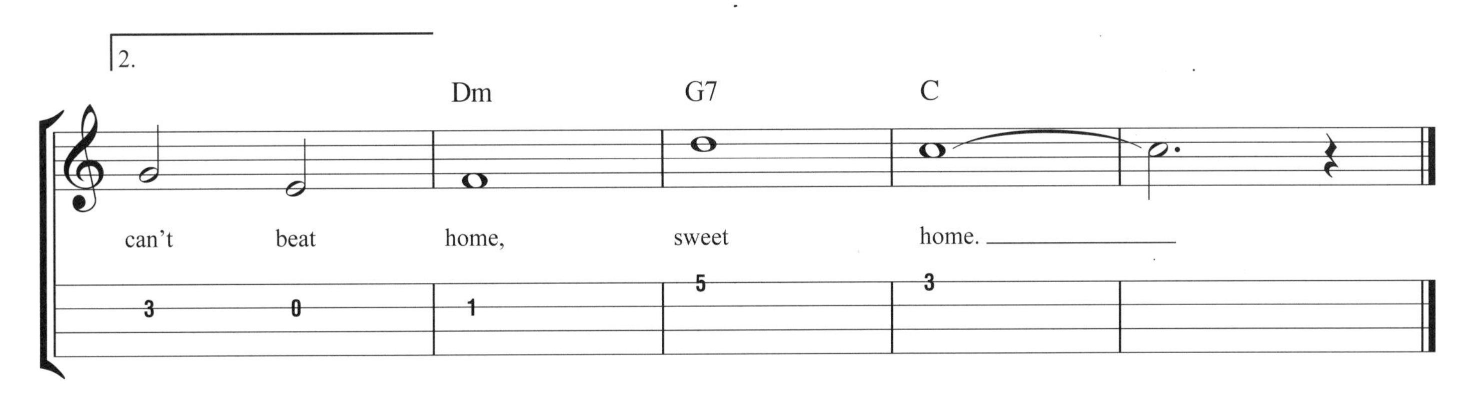
2.
Dm G7 C
can't beat home, sweet home.
3 0 1 5 3

Have Yourself a Merry Little Christmas

from MEET ME IN ST. LOUIS

Words and Music by Hugh Martin and Ralph Blane

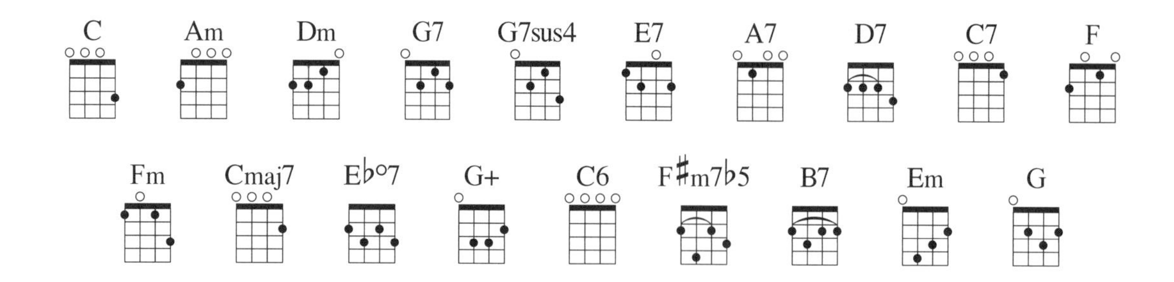

Verse

Moderately slow

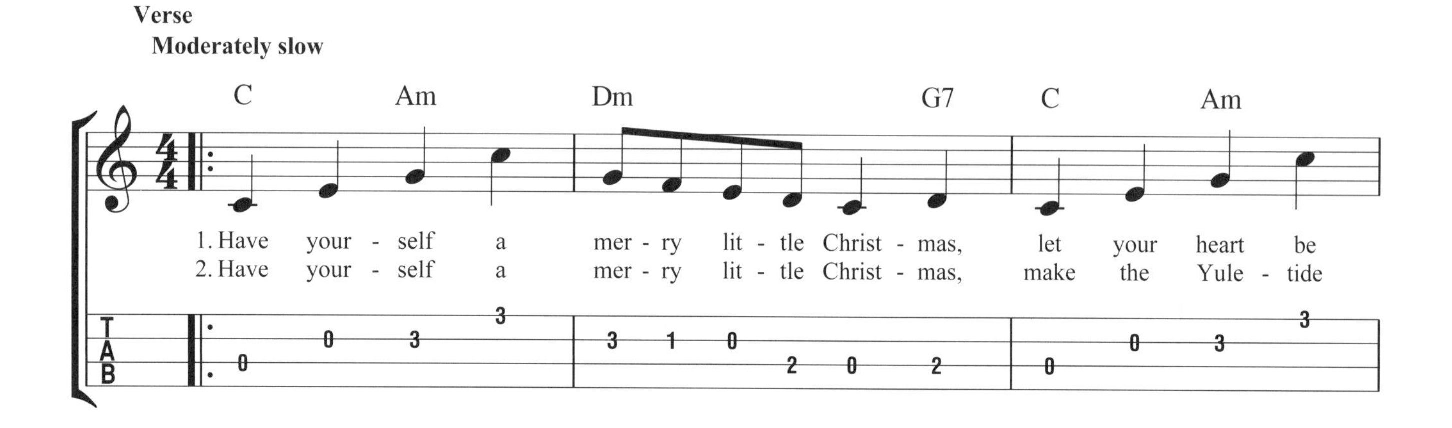

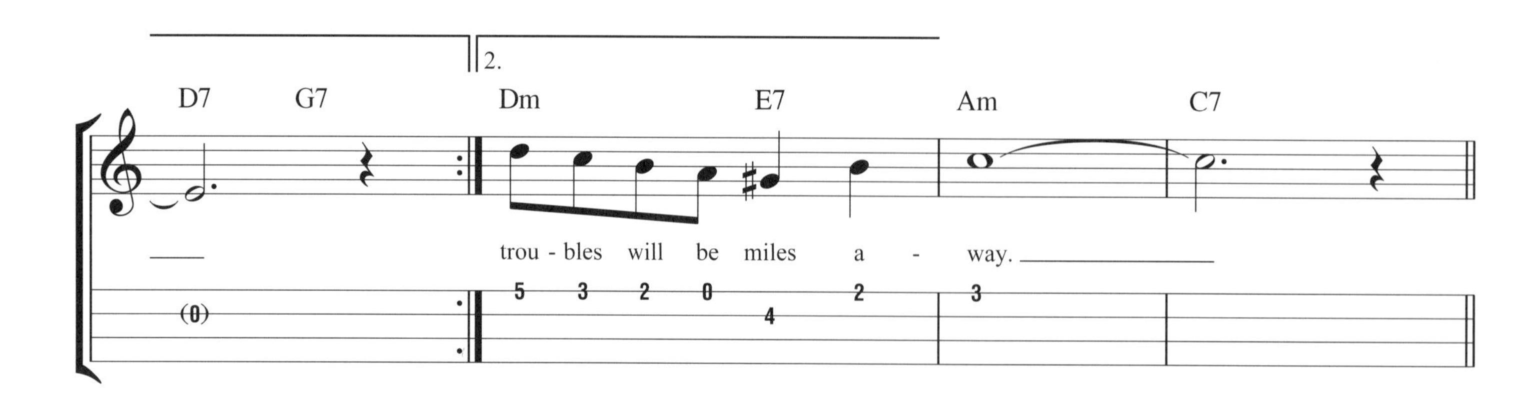

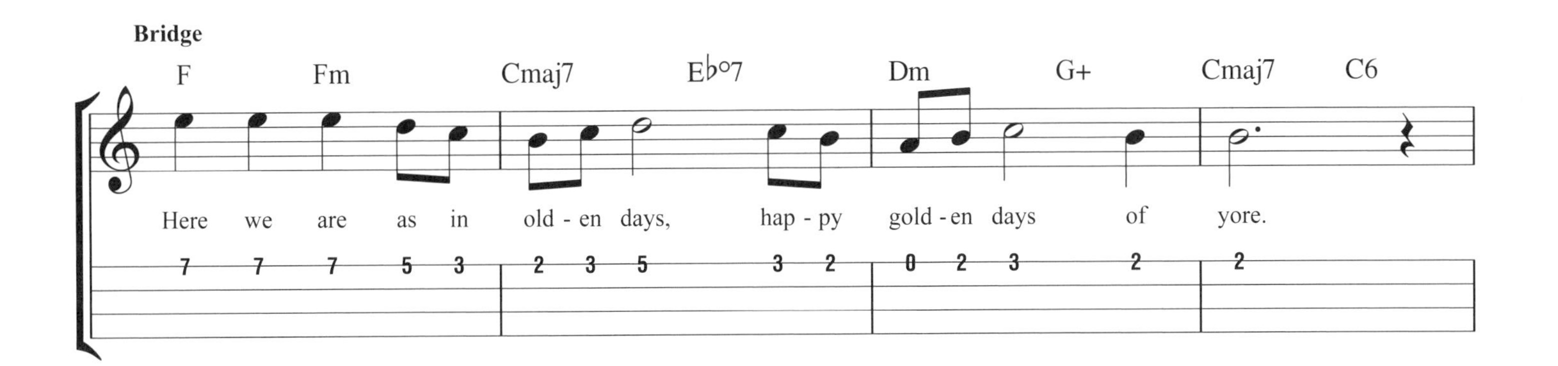
Bridge
F Fm Cmaj7 E♭°7 Dm G+ Cmaj7 C6
Here we are as in old - en days, hap - py gold - en days of yore.

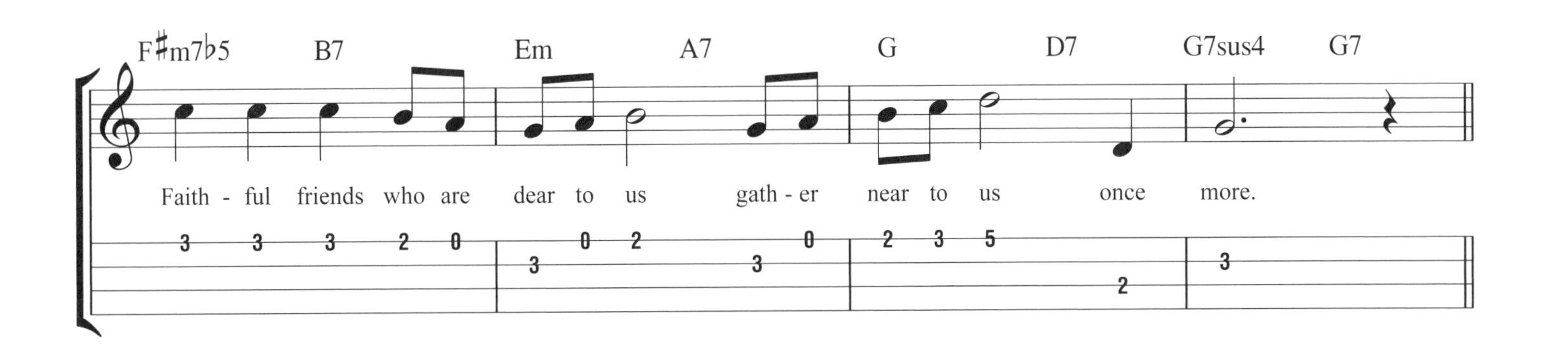
F♯m7♭5 B7 Em A7 G D7 G7sus4 G7
Faith - ful friends who are dear to us gath - er near to us once more.

Outro-Verse
C Am Dm G7 C Am G7sus4 G7
Through the years we all will be to - geth - er, if the fates al - low.

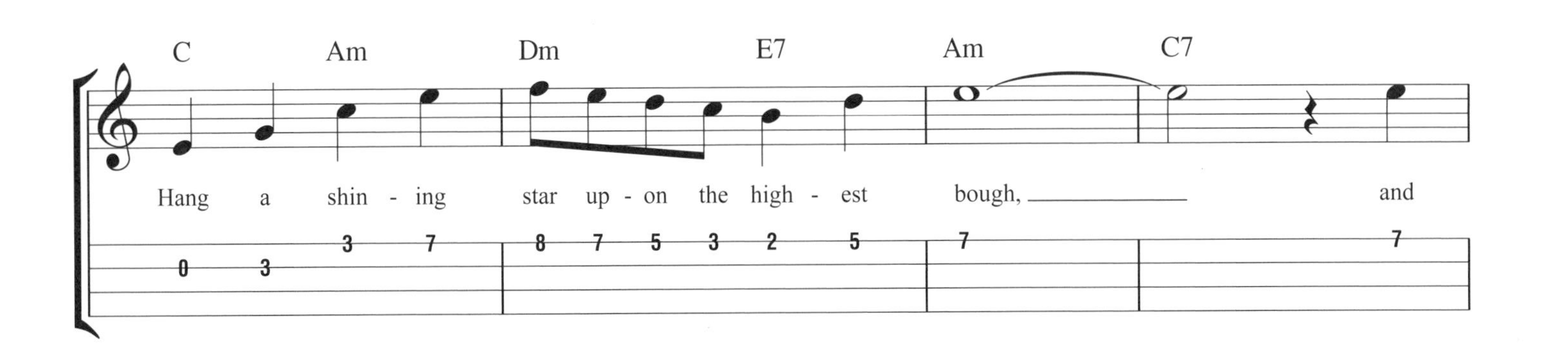
C Am Dm E7 Am C7
Hang a shin - ing star up - on the high - est bough, and

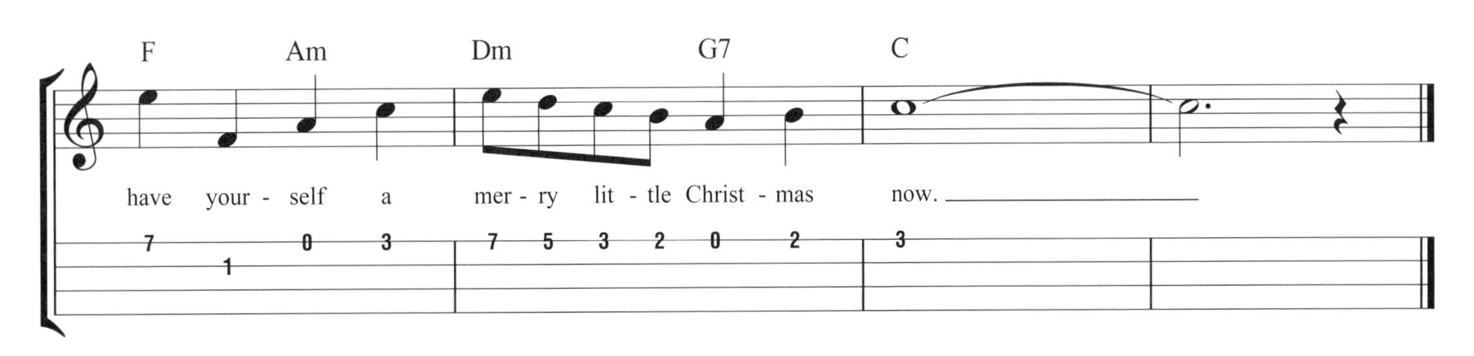
F Am Dm G7 C
have your - self a mer - ry lit - tle Christ - mas now.

Here Comes Santa Claus

(Right Down Santa Claus Lane)

Words and Music by Gene Autry and Oakley Haldeman

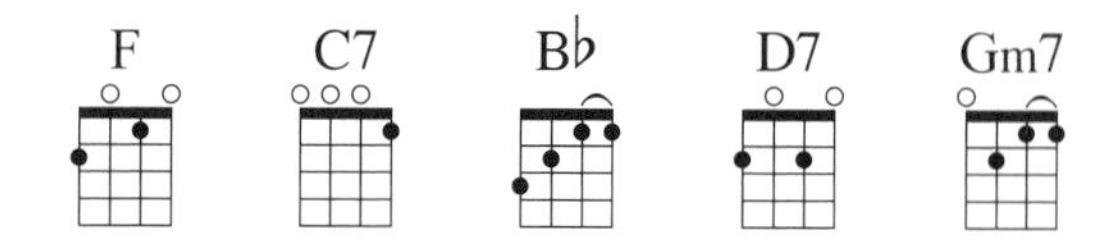

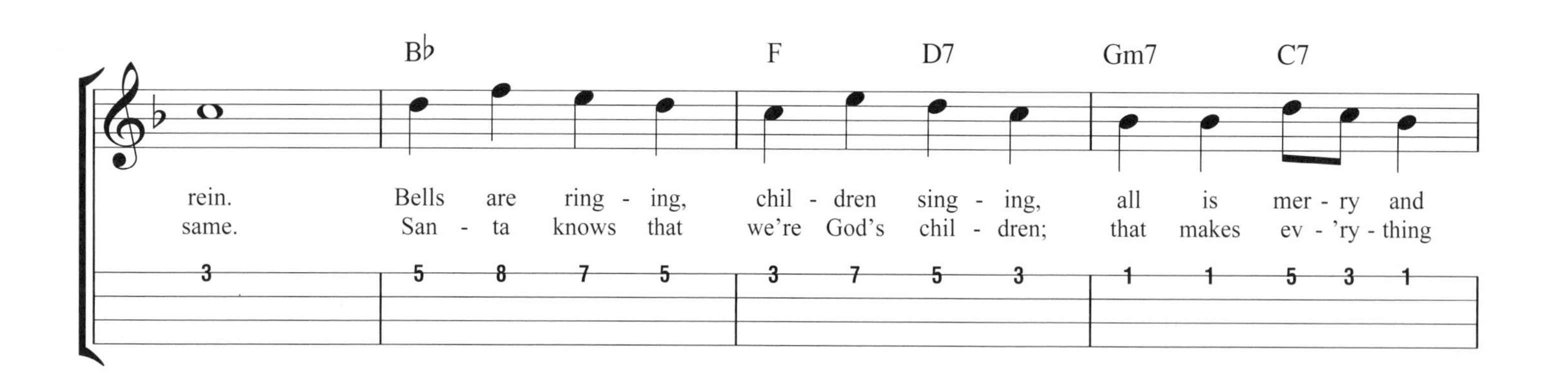

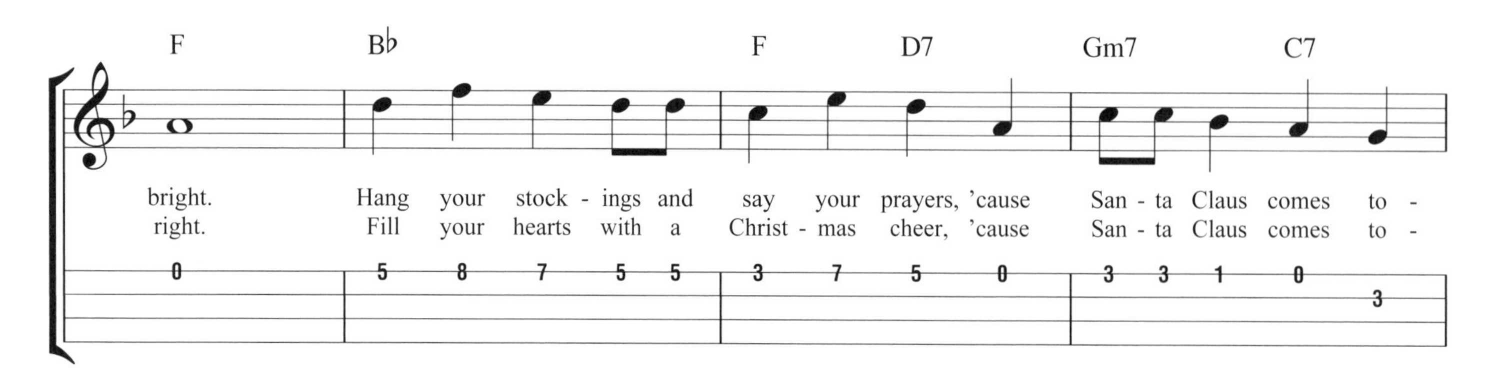

Verse
F C7 F
night. 2. Here comes San - ta Claus! Here comes San - ta Claus!
night. 4. Here comes San - ta Claus! Here comes San - ta Claus!

C7
Right down San - ta Claus Lane! He's got a bag that is filled with toys for the
Right down San - ta Claus Lane! He'll come a - round when the chimes ring out; then it's

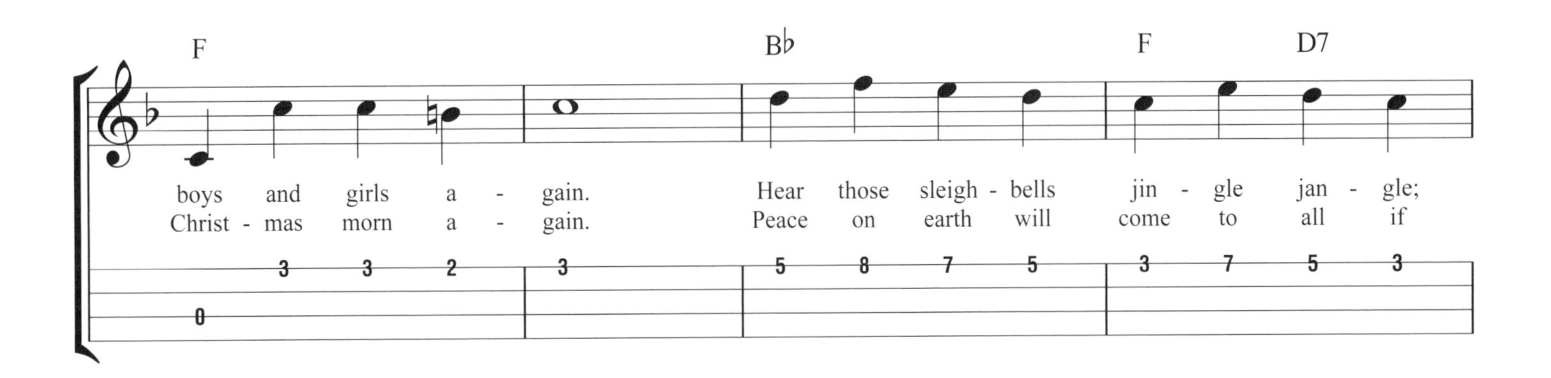
F Bb F D7
boys and girls a - gain. Hear those sleigh - bells jin - gle jan - gle;
Christ - mas morn a - gain. Peace on earth will come to all if

Gm7 C7 F Bb F D7
what a beau - ti - ful sight! Jump in bed, cov - er up your head, 'cause
we just fol - low the light. Let's give thanks to the Lord a - bove, 'cause

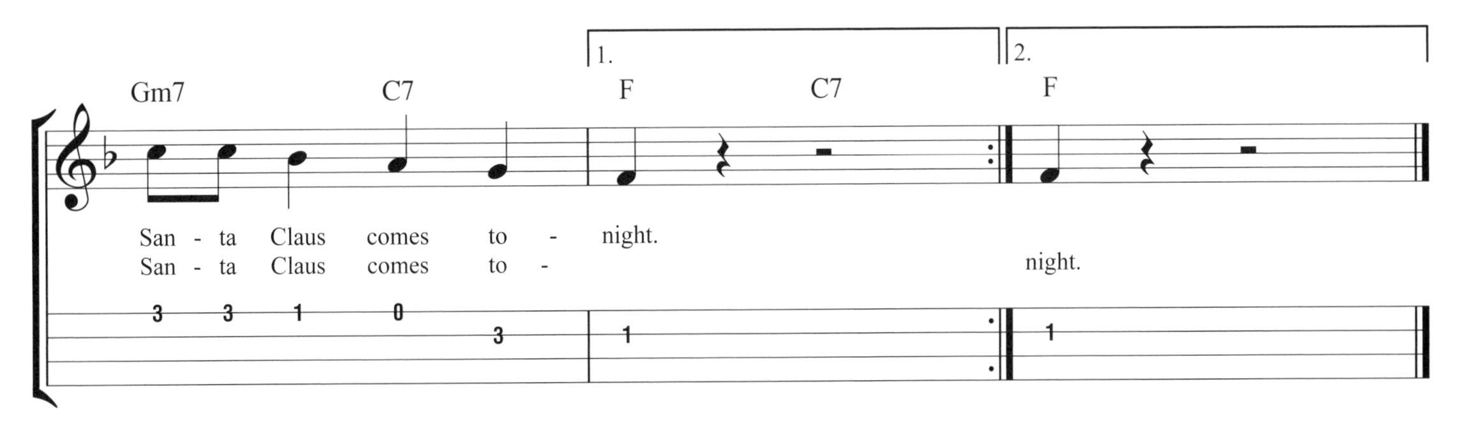
1. 2.
Gm7 C7 F C7 F
San - ta Claus comes to - night.
San - ta Claus comes to - night.

A Holly Jolly Christmas

Music and Lyrics by Johnny Marks

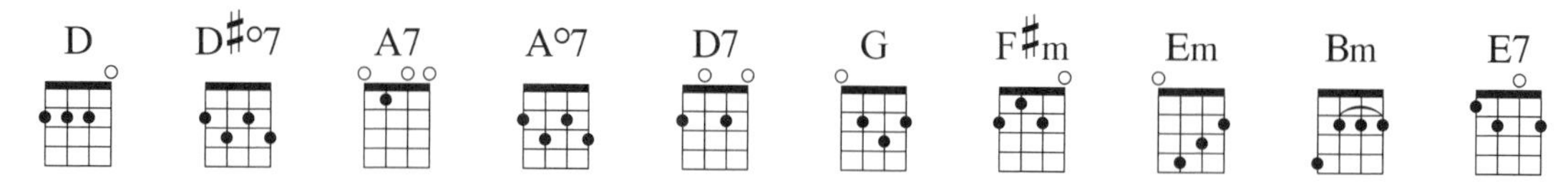

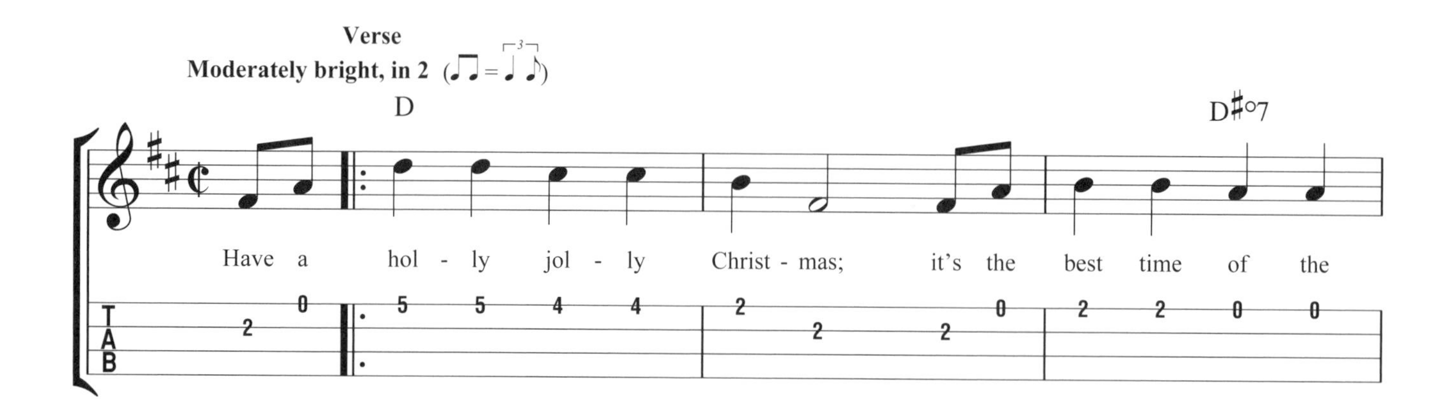

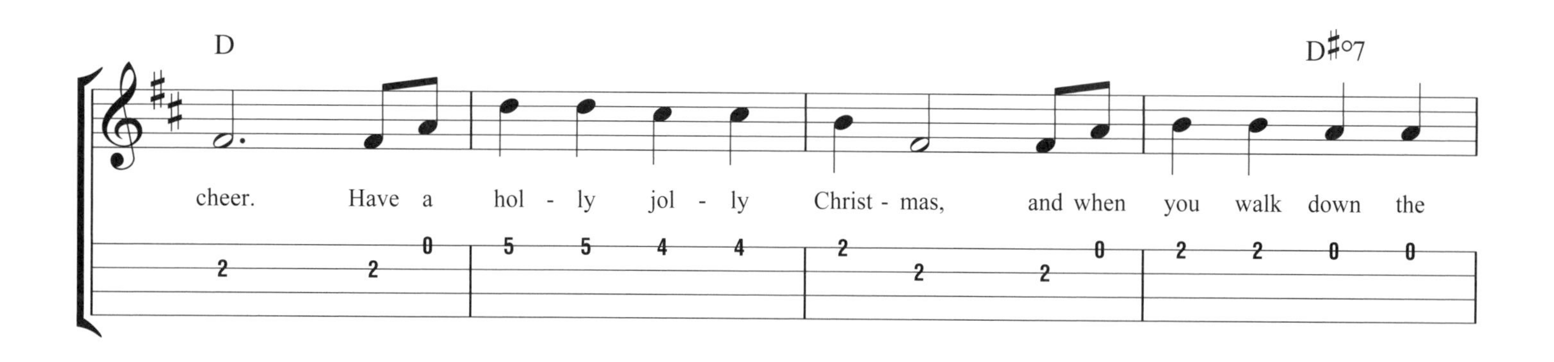

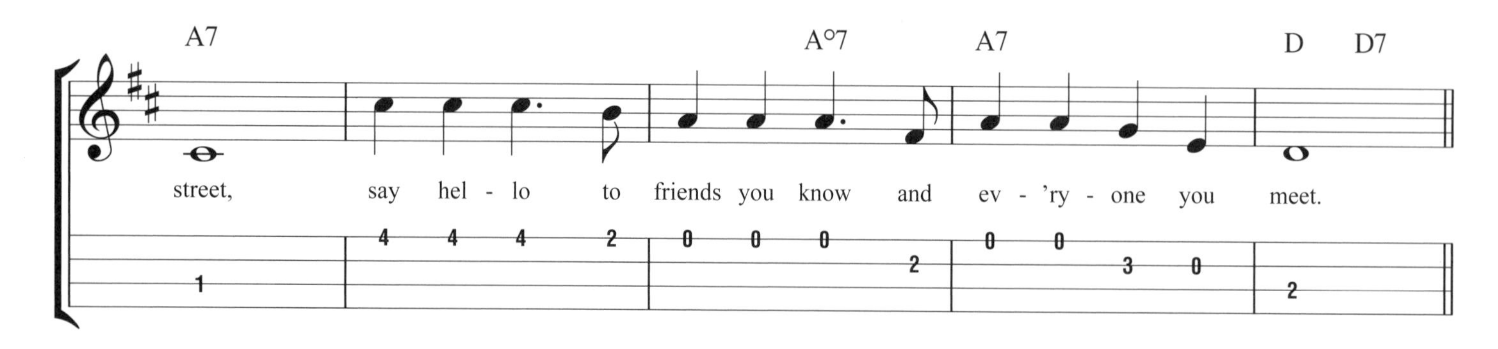

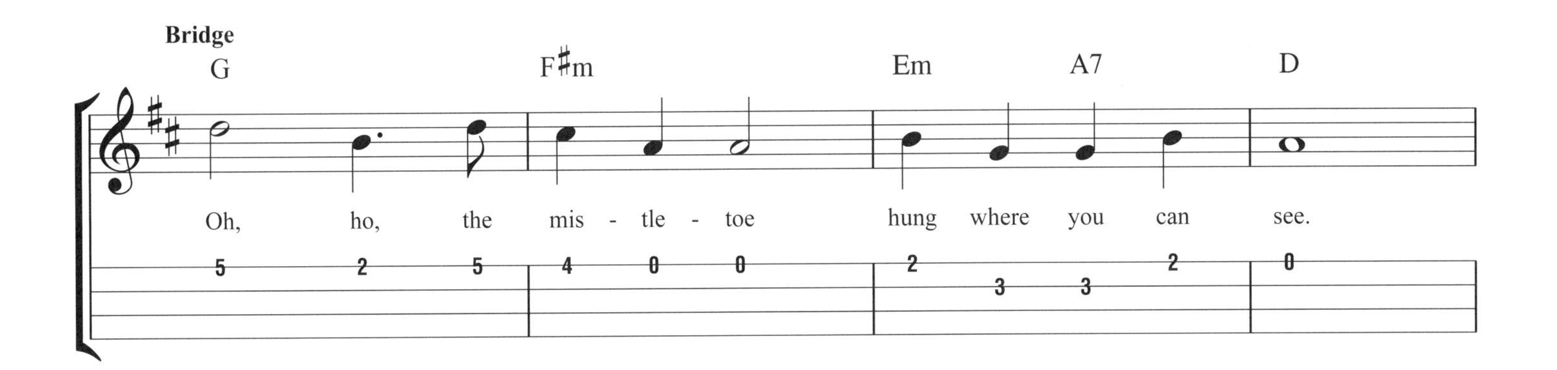
Bridge
G F♯m Em A7 D
Oh, ho, the mis - tle - toe hung where you can see.

Em Bm E7 A7
Some - bod - y waits for you; kiss her once for me. Have a

Outro-Verse
D D♯°7 A7
hol - ly jol - ly Christ - mas, and in case you did - n't hear,

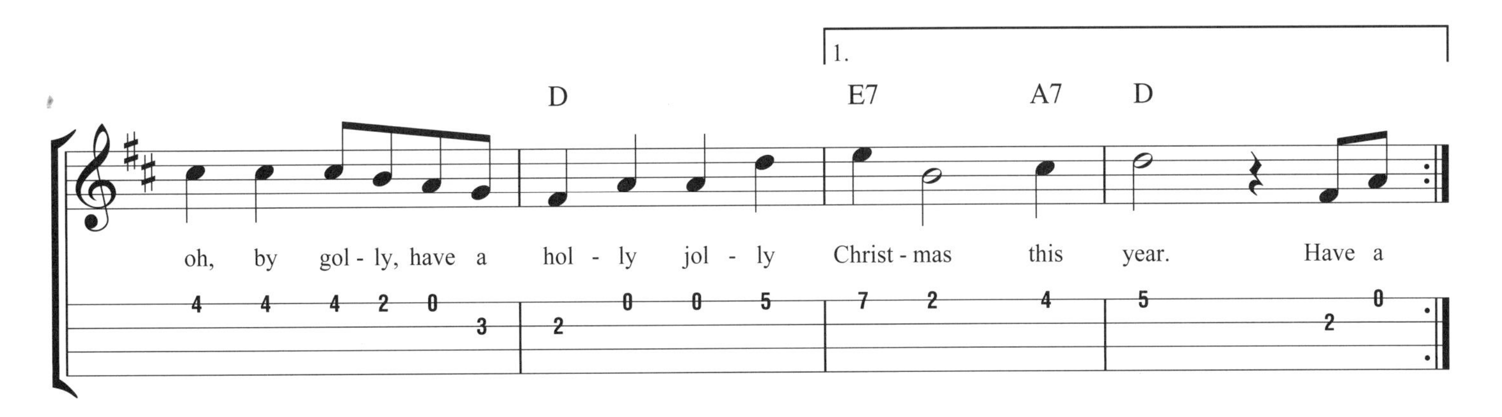
1.
D E7 A7 D
oh, by gol - ly, have a hol - ly jol - ly Christ - mas this year. Have a

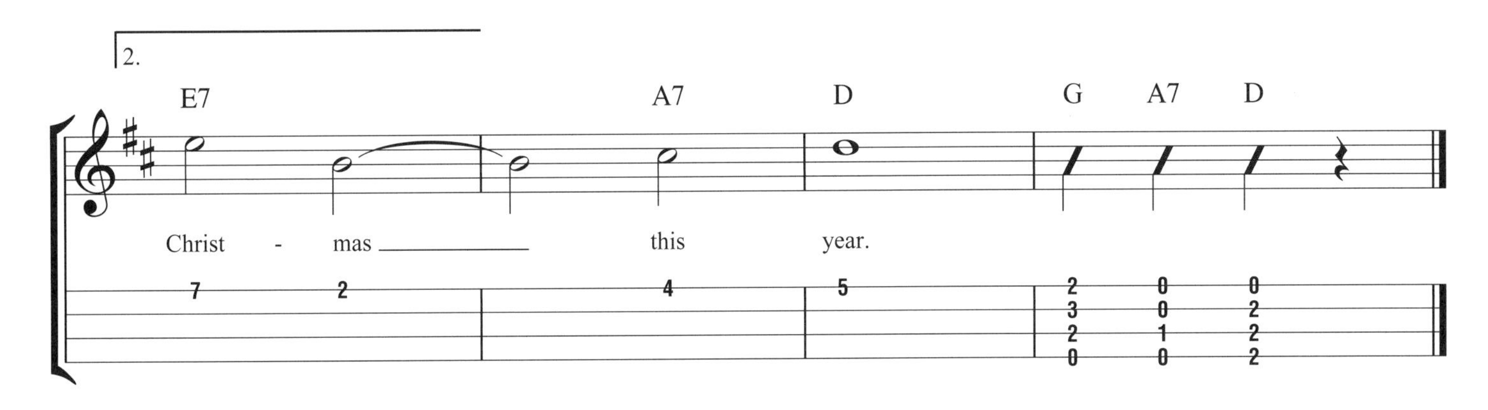
2.
E7 A7 D G A7 D
Christ - mas this year.

I Heard the Bells on Christmas Day

Words by Henry Wadsworth Longfellow
Adapted by Johnny Marks
Music by Johnny Marks

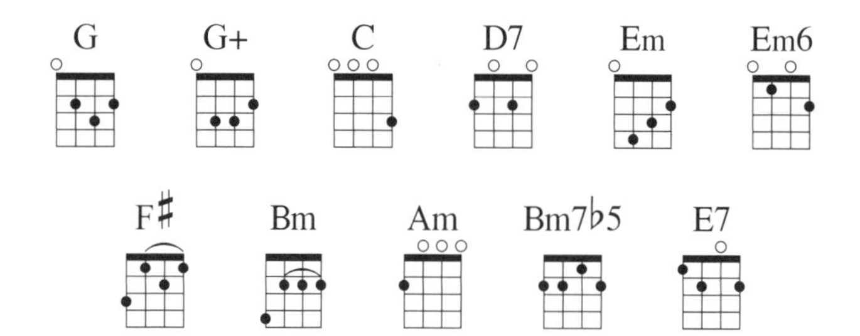

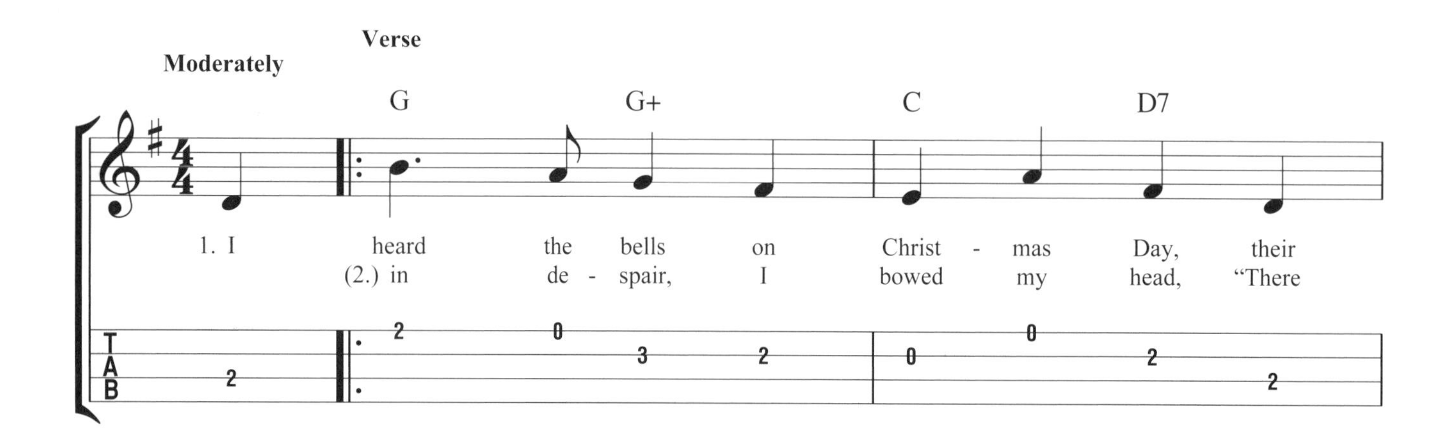

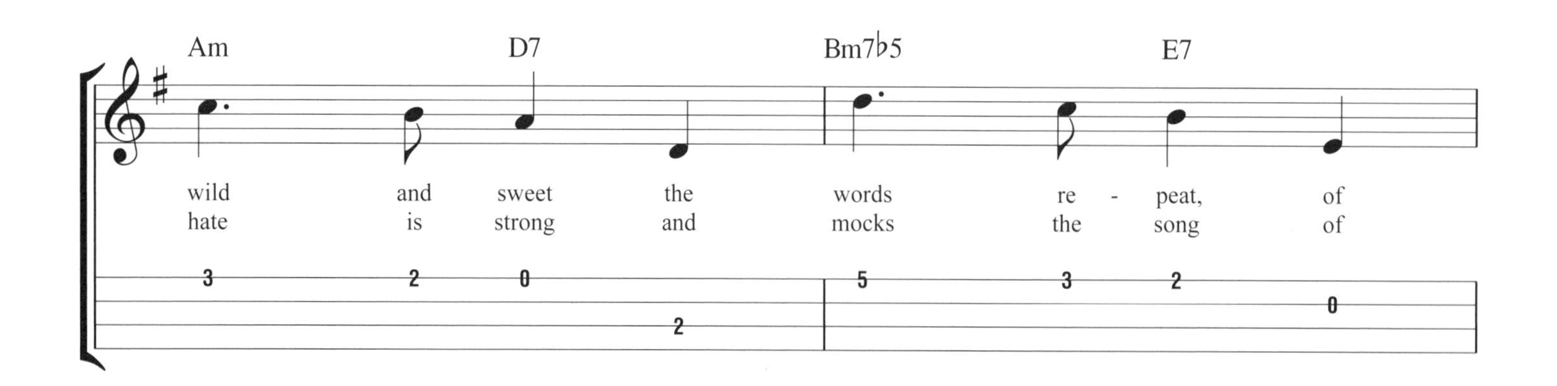

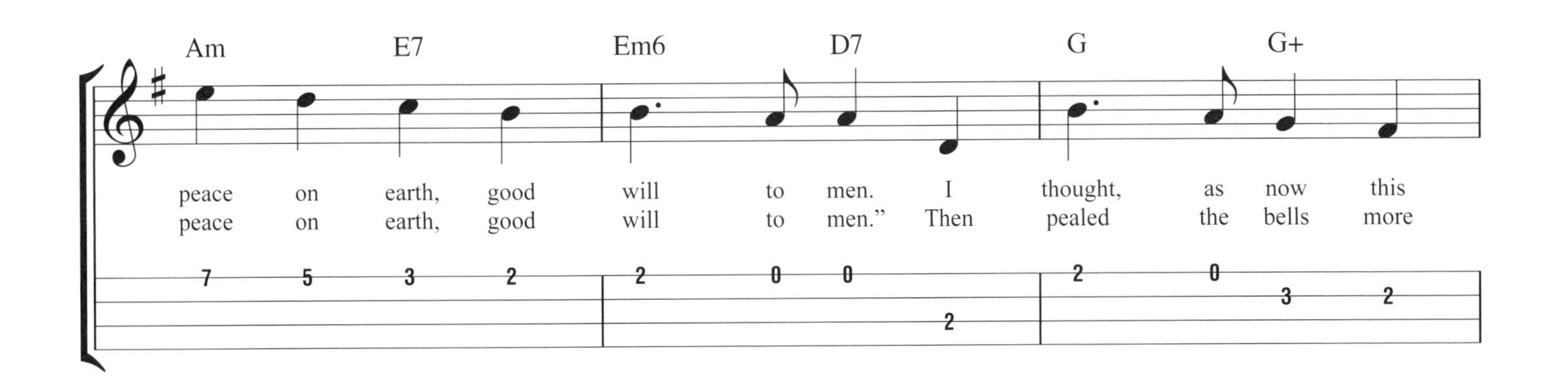
Am E7 Em6 D7 G G+
peace on earth, good will to men. I thought, as now this
peace on earth, good will to men." Then pealed the bells more

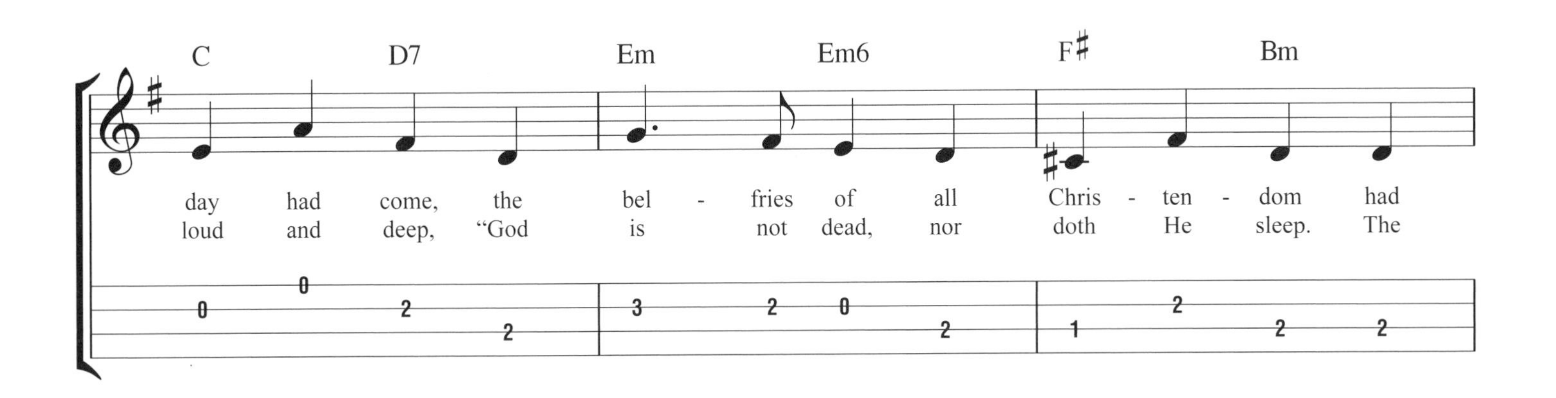
C D7 Em Em6 F♯ Bm
day had come, the bel - fries of all Chris - ten - dom had
loud and deep, "God is not dead, nor doth He sleep. The

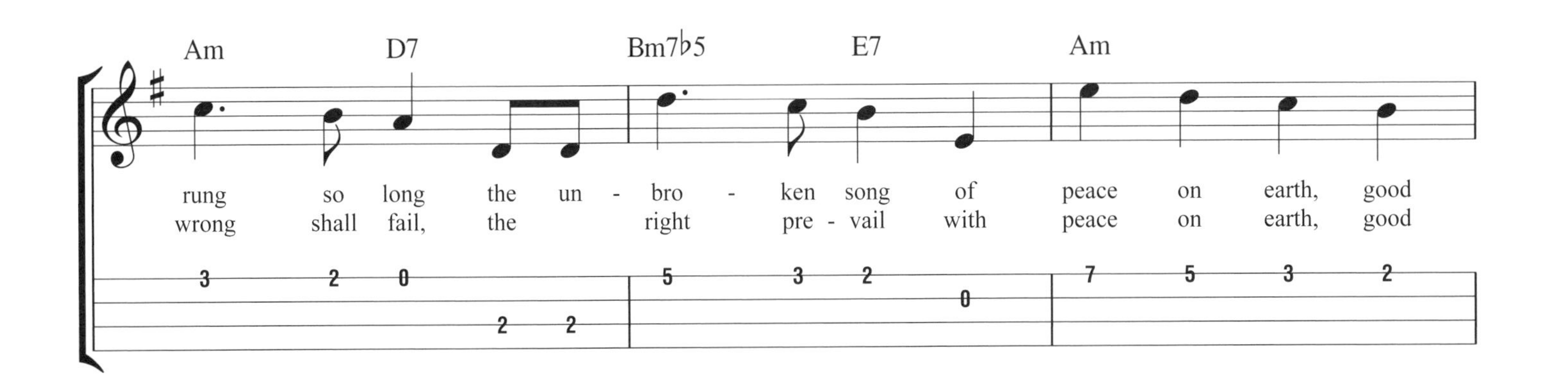
Am D7 Bm7♭5 E7 Am
rung so long the un - bro - ken song of peace on earth, good
wrong shall fail, the right pre - vail with peace on earth, good

1.
2.
D7 G D7 G
will to men. 2. And will to men."

I'll Be Home for Christmas

Words and Music by Kim Gannon and Walter Kent

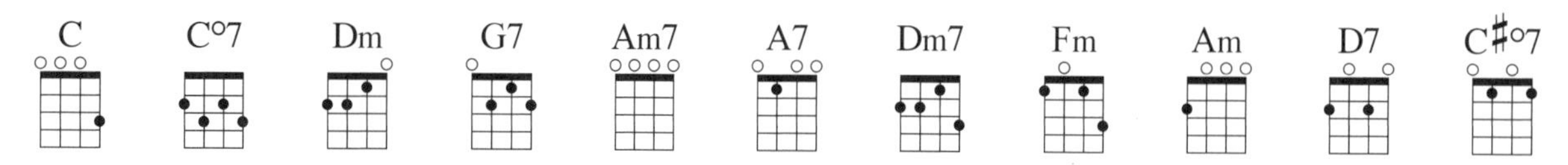

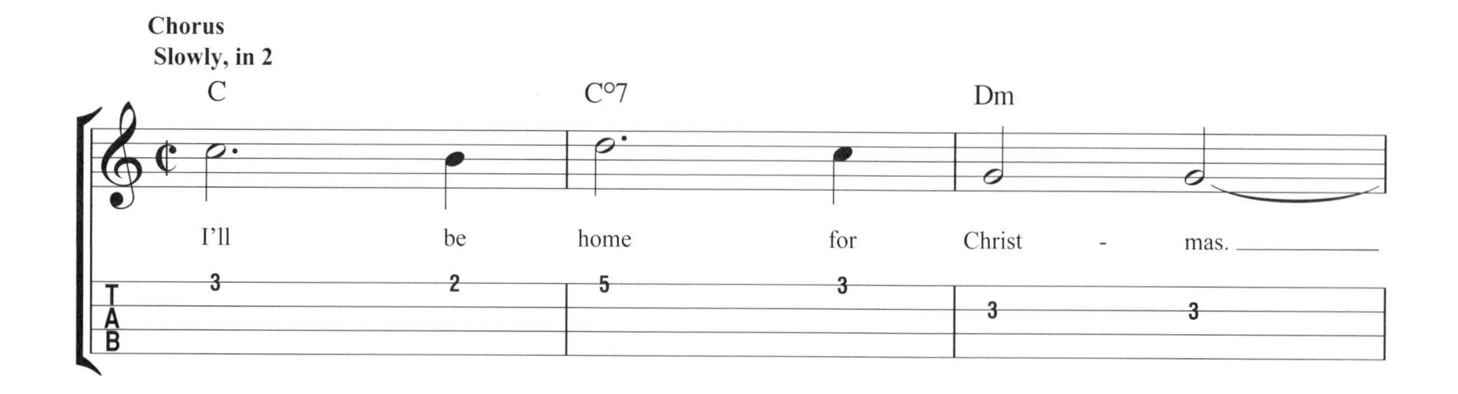

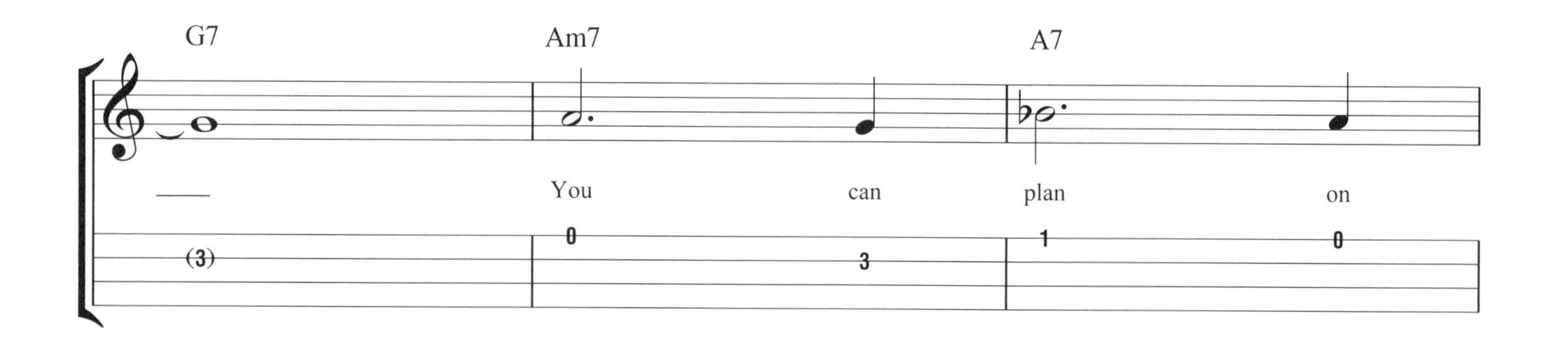

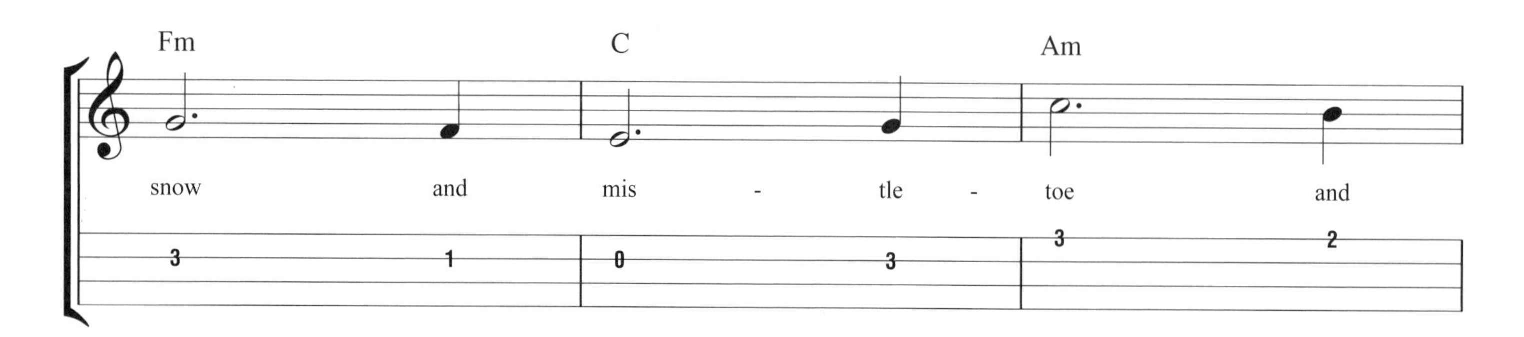

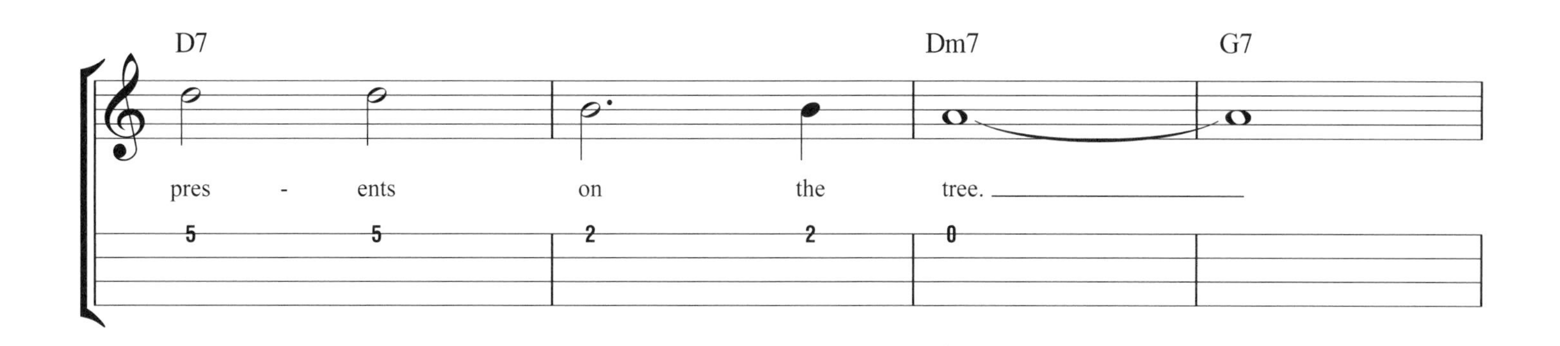
D7
Dm7
G7
pres - ents on the tree.
5 5 2 2 0

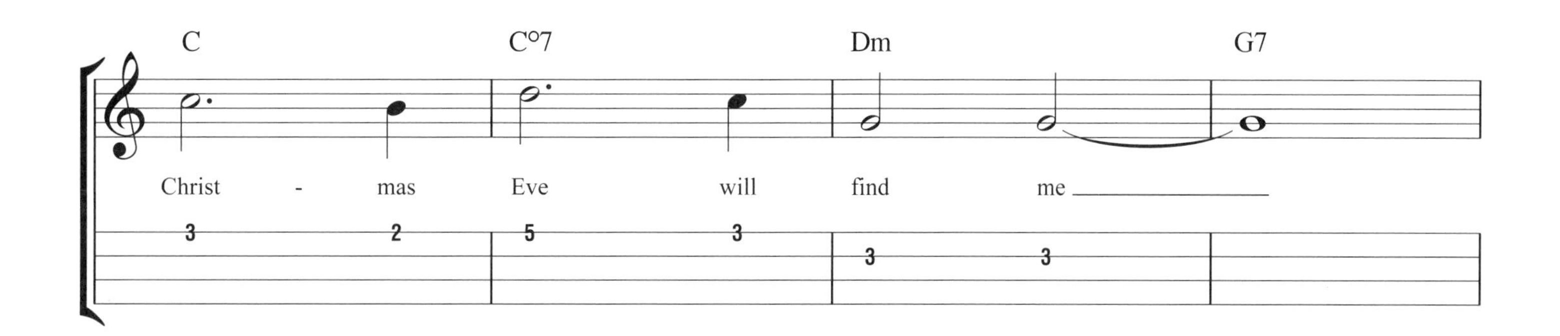
C
C°7
Dm
G7
Christ - mas Eve will find me
3 2 5 3 3 3

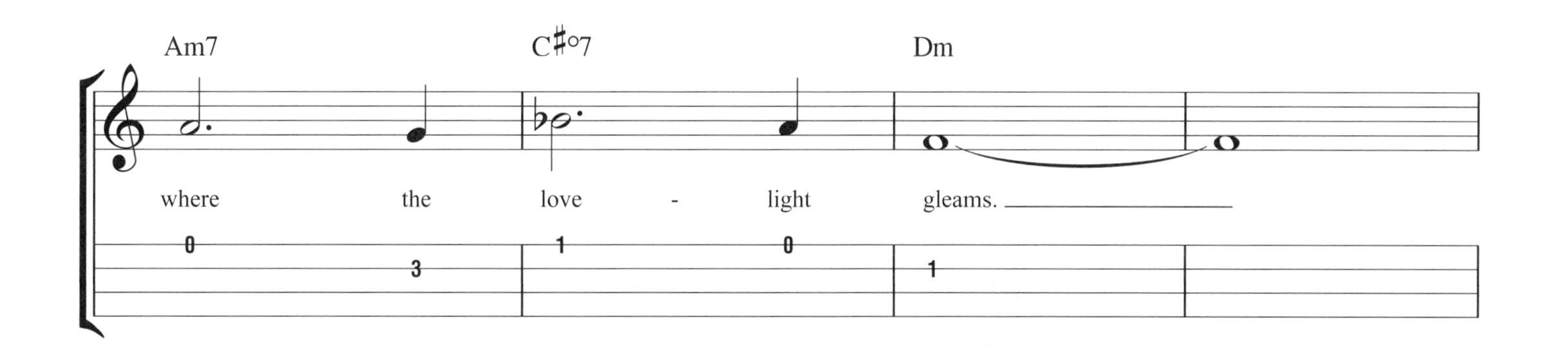
Am7
C♯°7
Dm
where the love - light gleams.
0 3 1 0 1

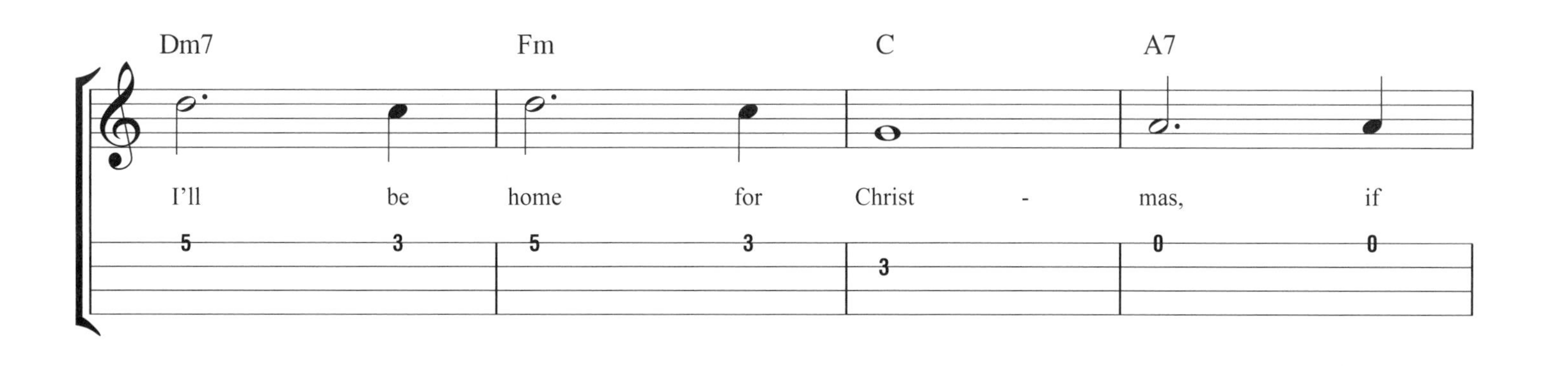
Dm7
Fm
C
A7
I'll be home for Christ - mas, if
5 3 5 3 3 0 0

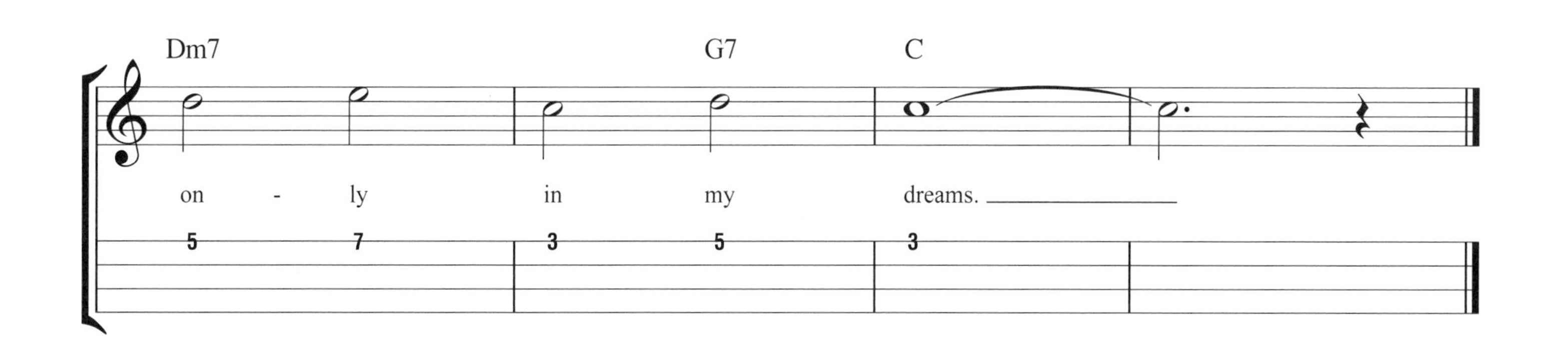
Dm7
G7
C
on - ly in my dreams.
5 7 3 5 3

Jingle Bell Rock

Words and Music by Joe Beal and Jim Boothe

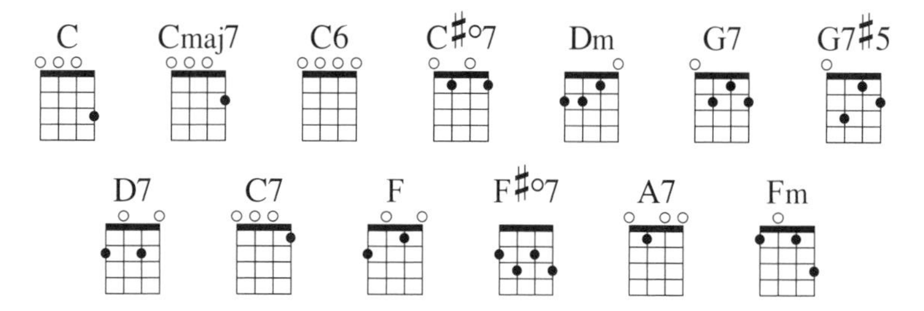

Verse
Moderately bright

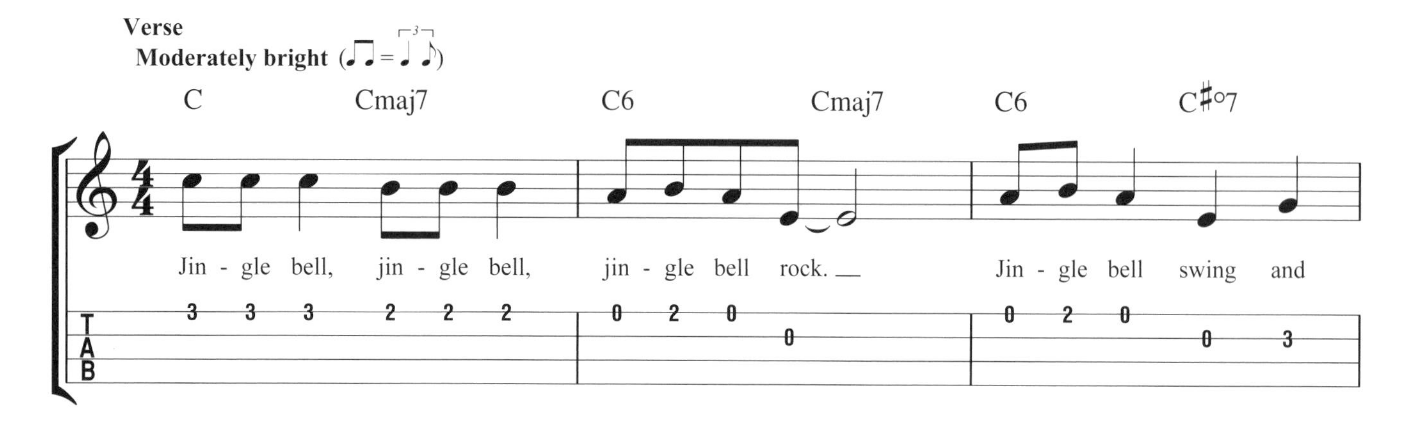

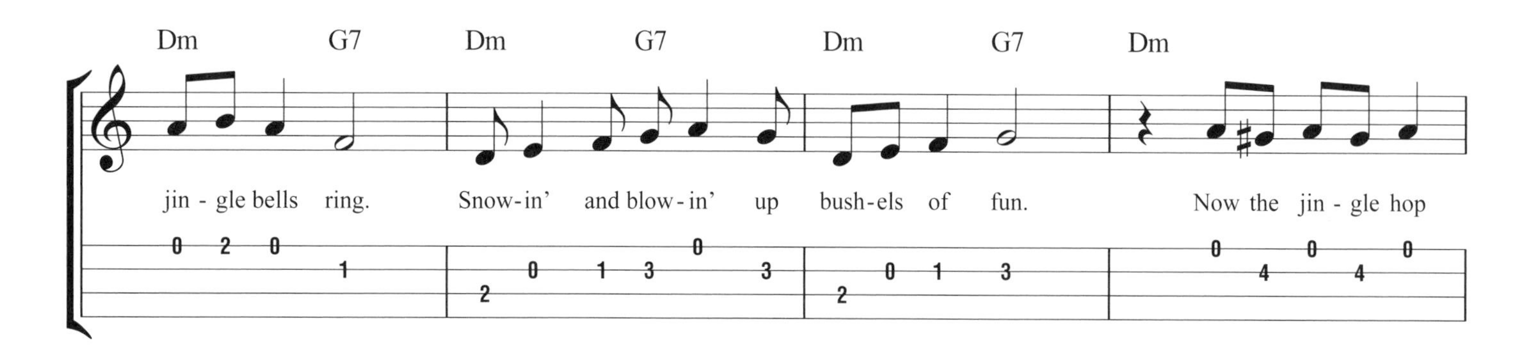

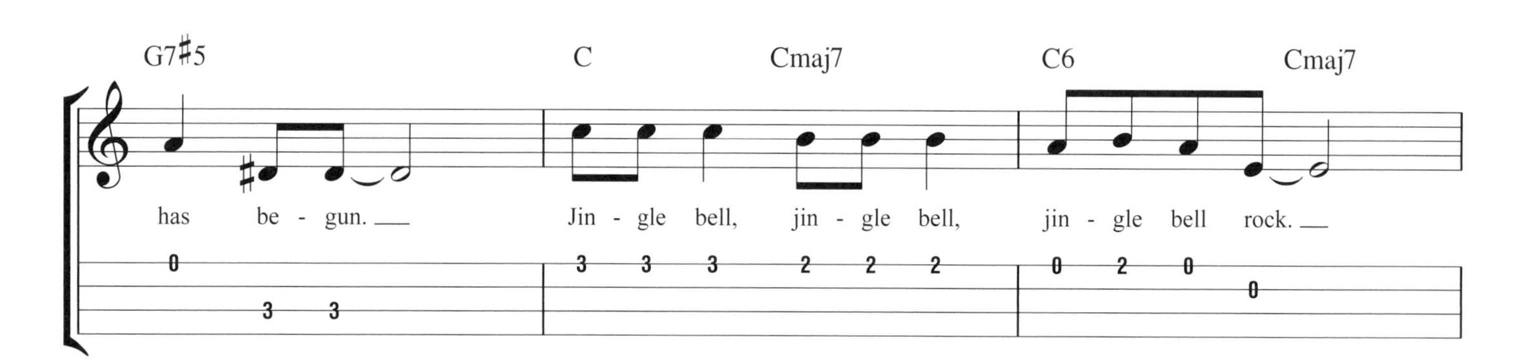

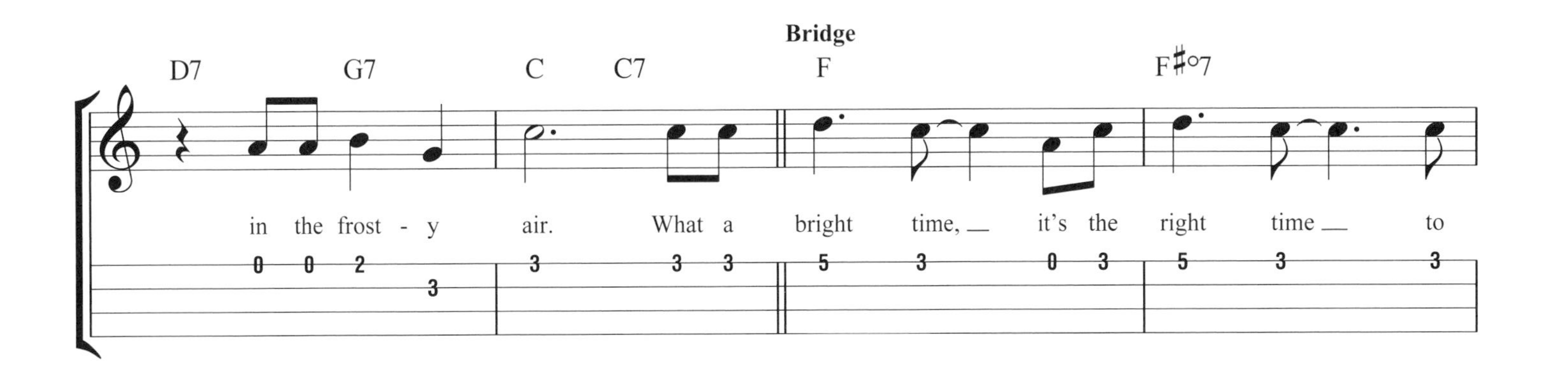
Bridge
D7 G7 C C7 F F♯°7
in the frost - y air. What a bright time, it's the right time to

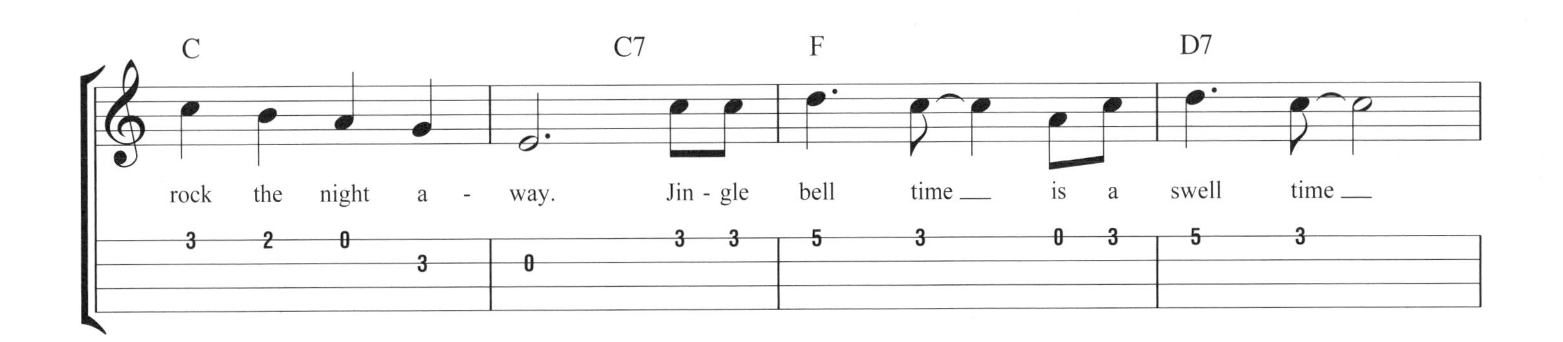
C C7 F D7
rock the night a - way. Jin - gle bell time is a swell time

Outro-Verse
G7 C Cmaj7 C6 Cmaj7
to go glid-in' in a one-horse sleigh. Gid-dy-ap, jin-gle horse, pick up your feet,

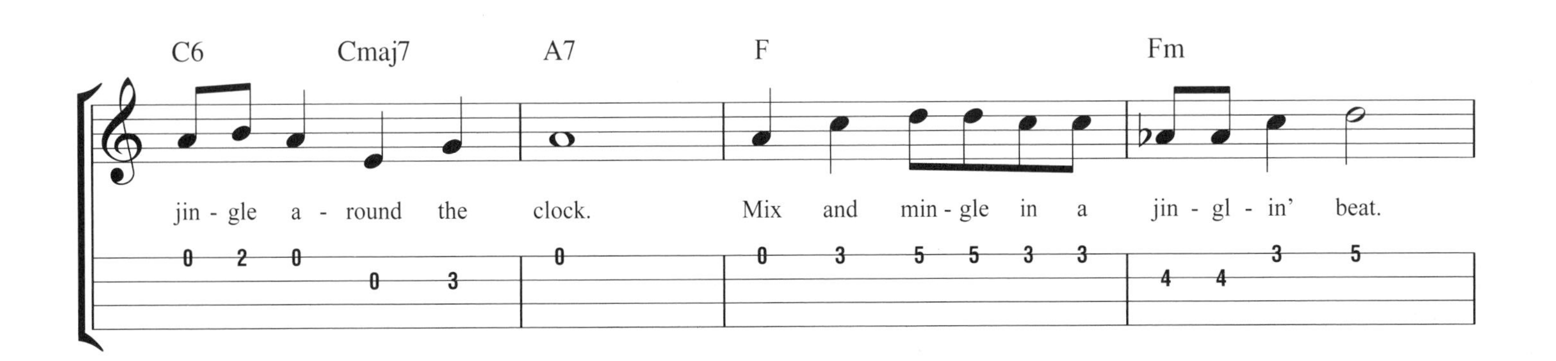
C6 Cmaj7 A7 F Fm
jin - gle a - round the clock. Mix and min - gle in a jin - gl - in' beat.

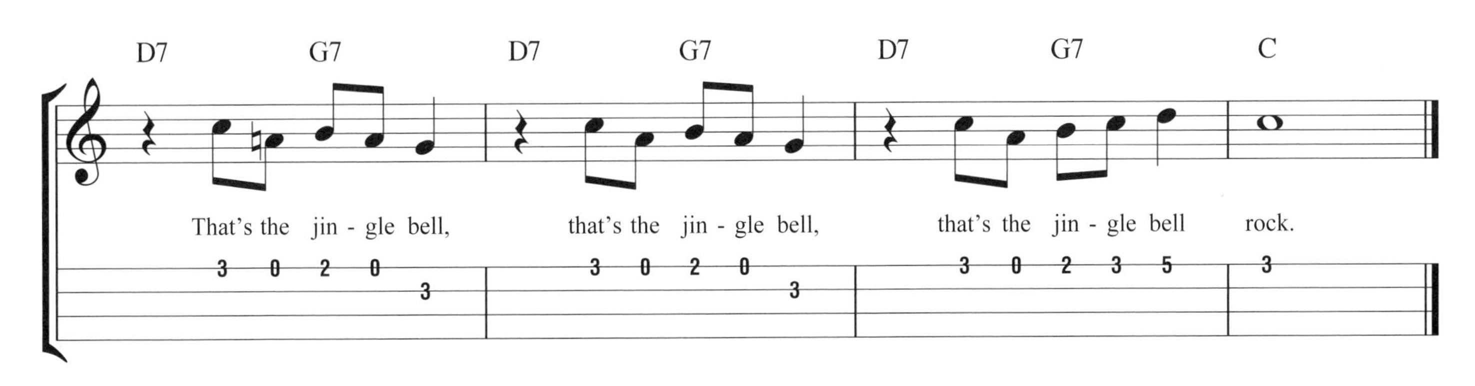
D7 G7 D7 G7 D7 G7 C
That's the jin - gle bell, that's the jin - gle bell, that's the jin - gle bell rock.

Let It Snow! Let It Snow! Let It Snow!

Words by Sammy Cahn
Music by Jule Styne

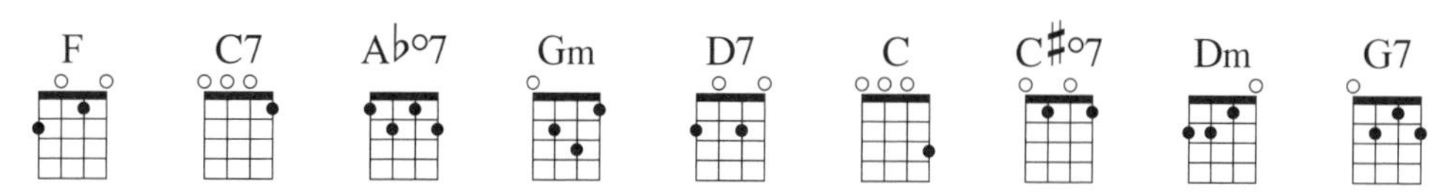

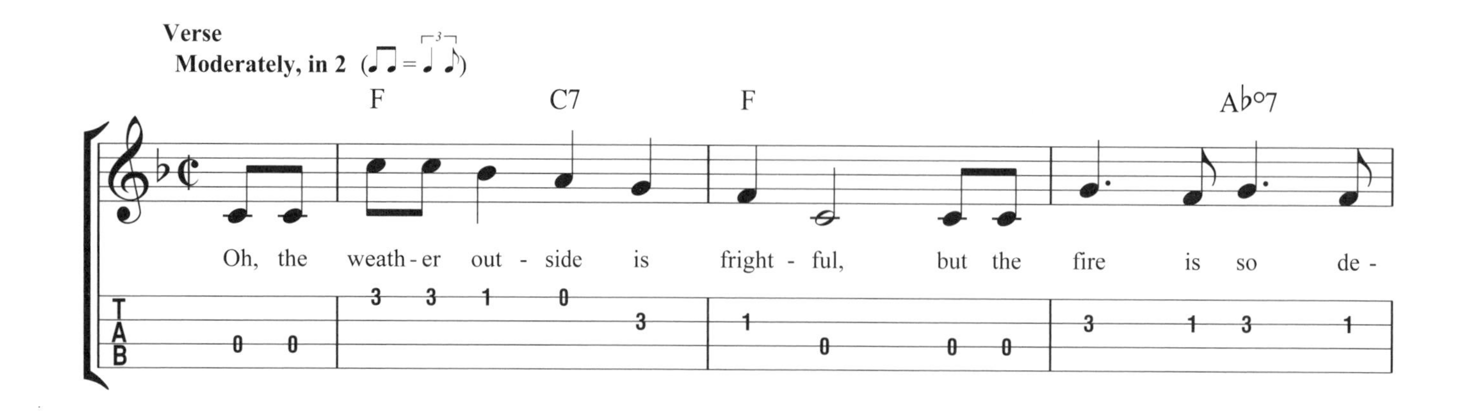

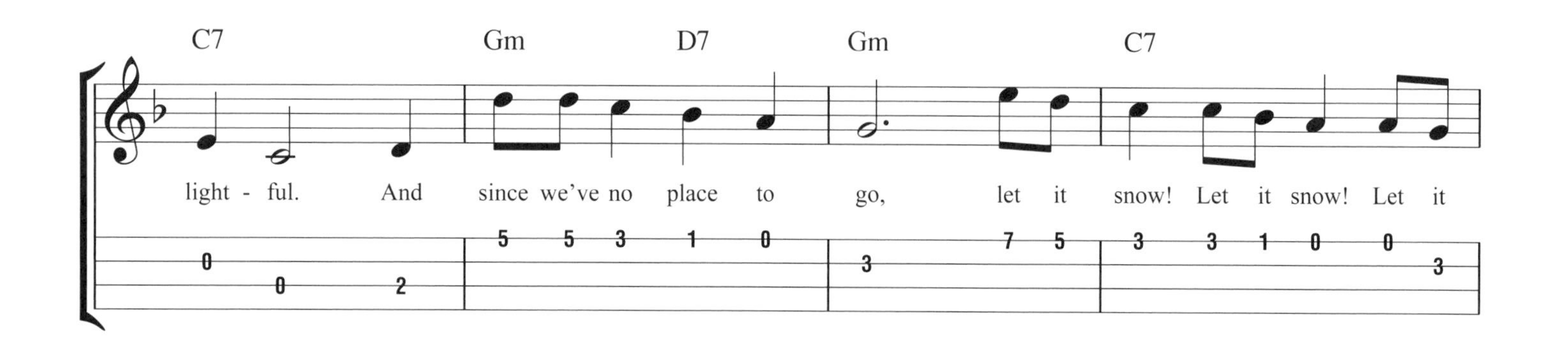

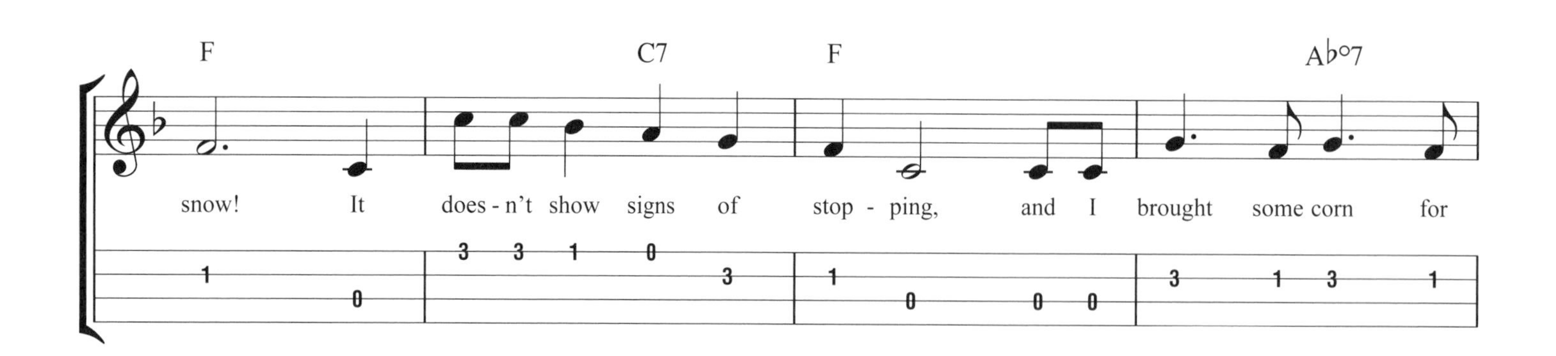

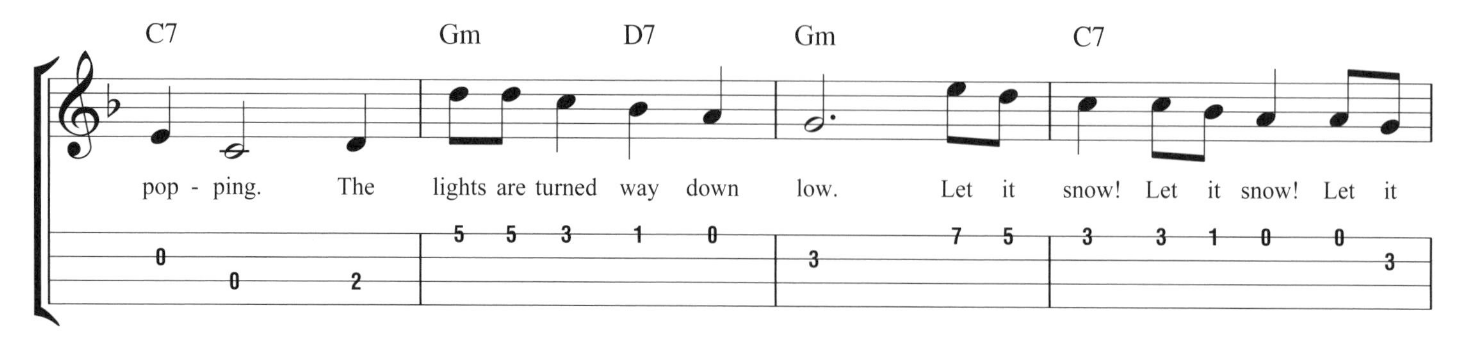

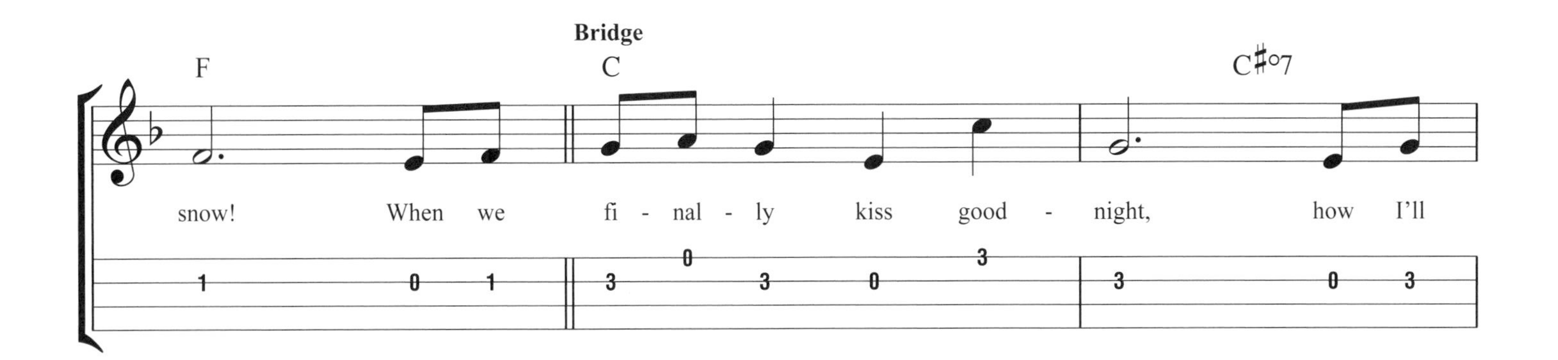
Bridge
F C C♯°7
snow! When we fi - nal - ly kiss good - night, how I'll

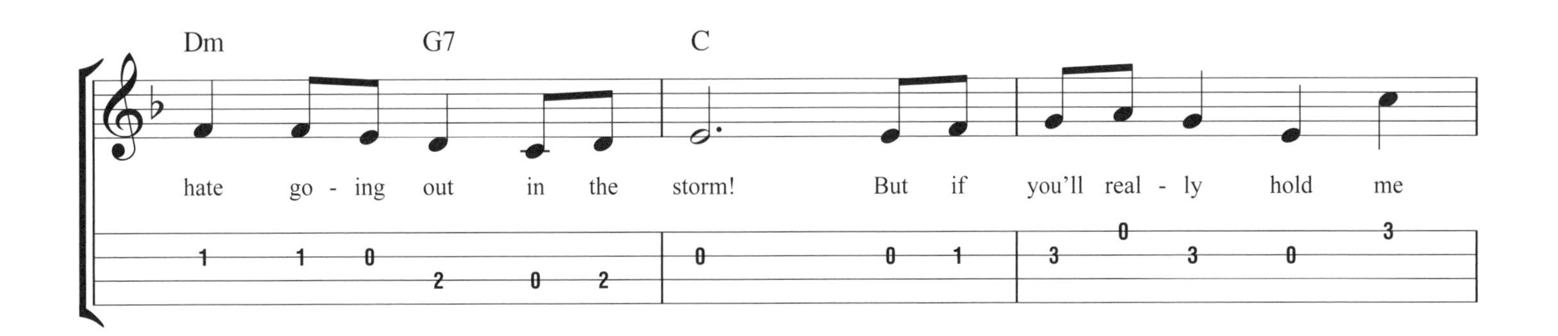
Dm G7 C
hate go - ing out in the storm! But if you'll real - ly hold me

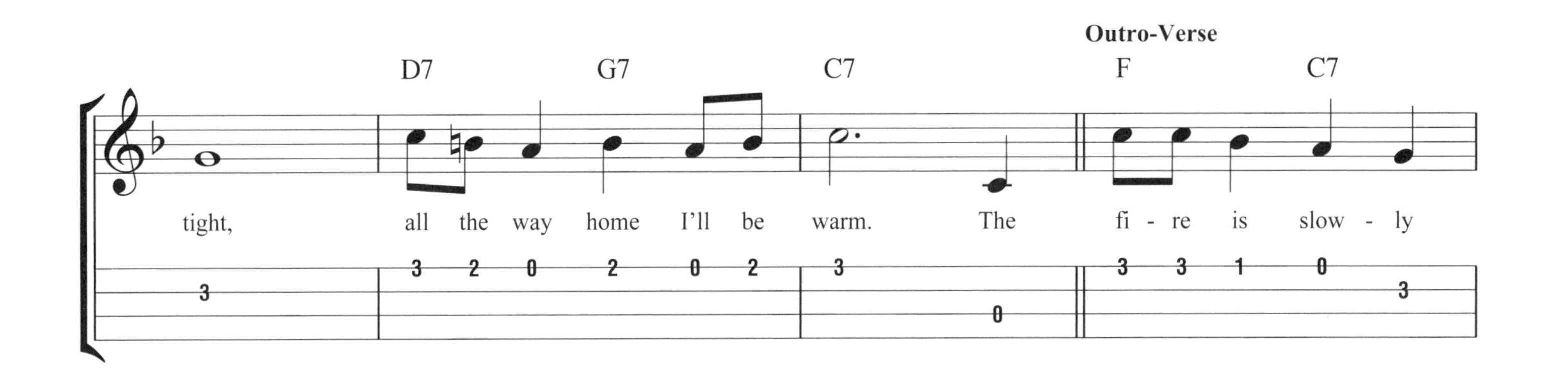
Outro-Verse
D7 G7 C7 F C7
tight, all the way home I'll be warm. The fi - re is slow - ly

F A♭°7 C7
dy - ing, and my dear, we're still good - bye - ing. But as

Gm D7 Gm C7 F
long as you love me so, let it snow! Let it snow! Let it snow!

The Little Drummer Boy

Words and Music by Harry Simeone, Henry Onorati and Katherine Davis

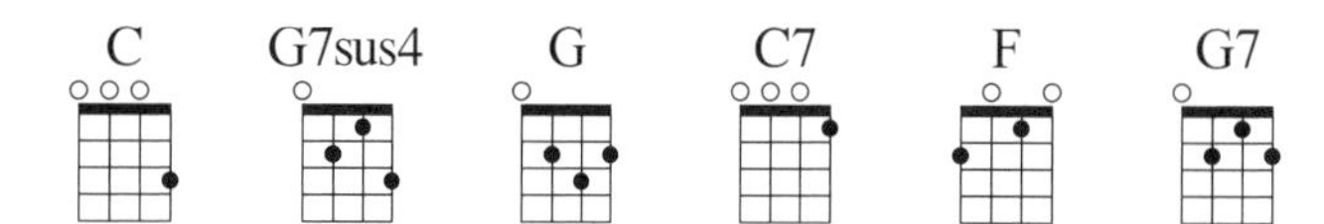

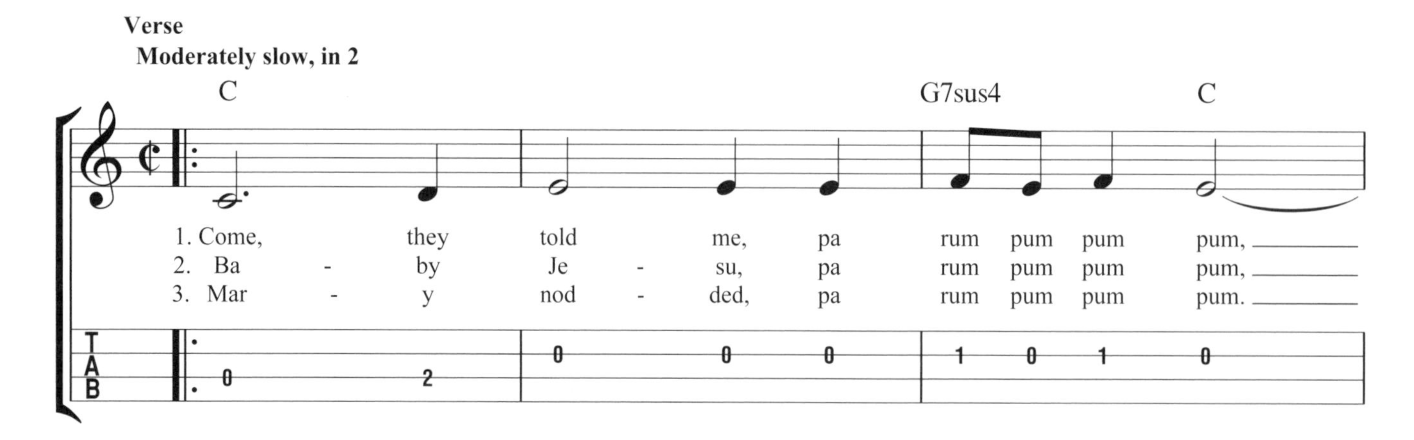

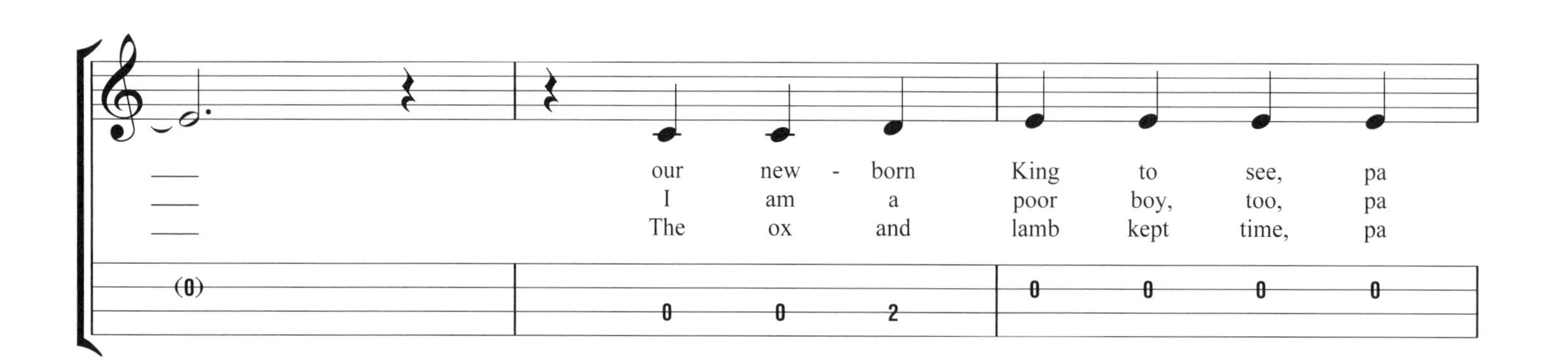

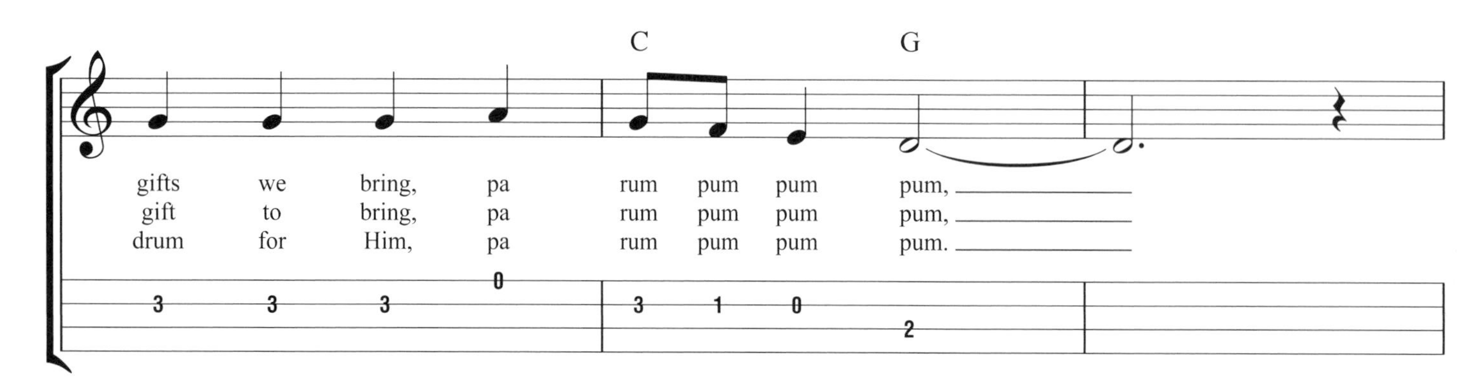

C C7 F
to lay be - fore the King, pa rum pum pum pum,
that's fit to give our King, pa rum pum pum pum,
I played my best for Him, pa rum pum pum pum,

C G
rum pum pum pum, rum pum pum pum,
rum pum pum pum, rum pum pum pum.
rum pum pum pum, rum pum pum pum.

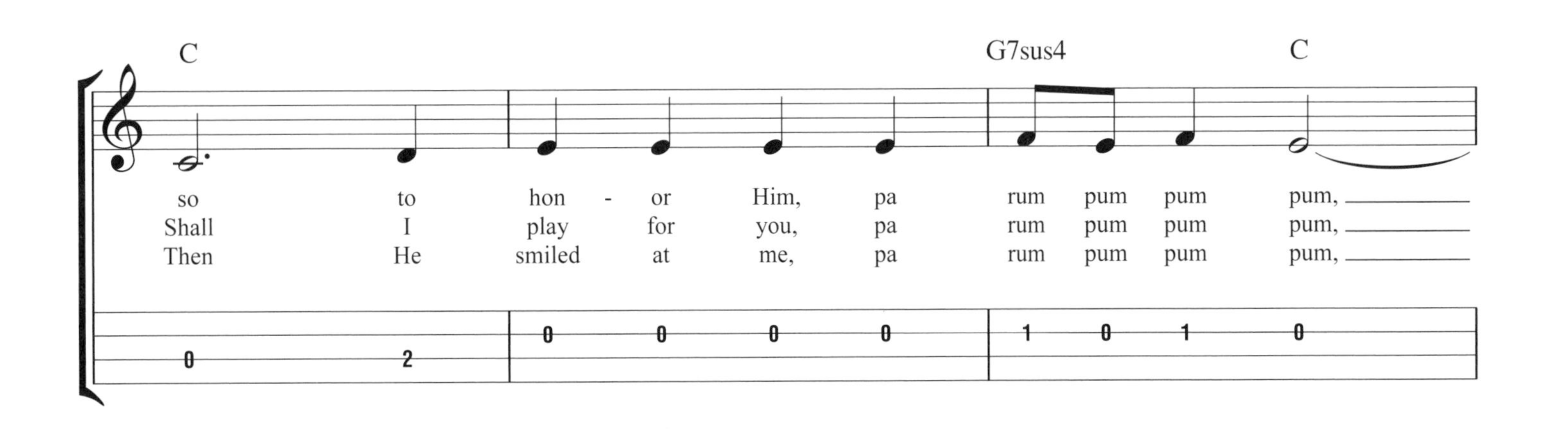
C G7sus4 C
so to hon - or Him, pa rum pum pum pum,
Shall I play for you, pa rum pum pum pum,
Then He smiled at me, pa rum pum pum pum,

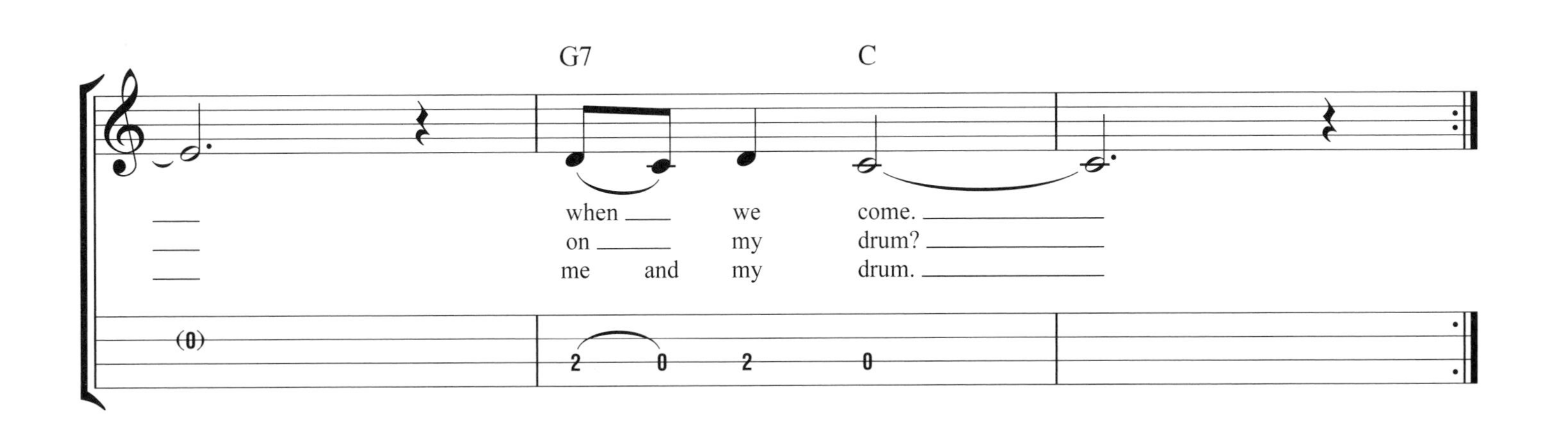
G7 C
when we come.
on my drum?
me and my drum.

The Most Wonderful Time of the Year

Words and Music by Eddie Pola and George Wyle

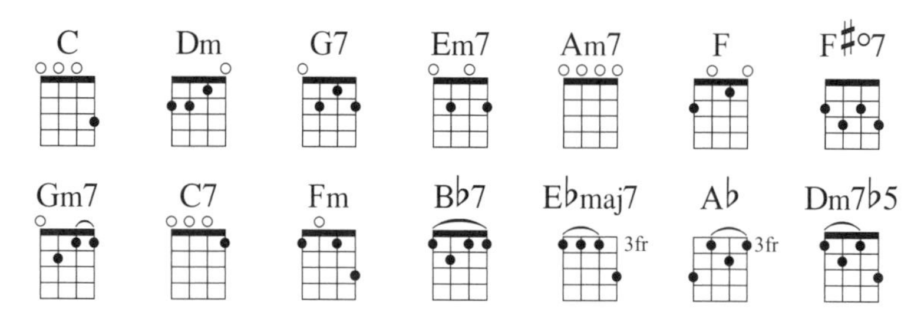

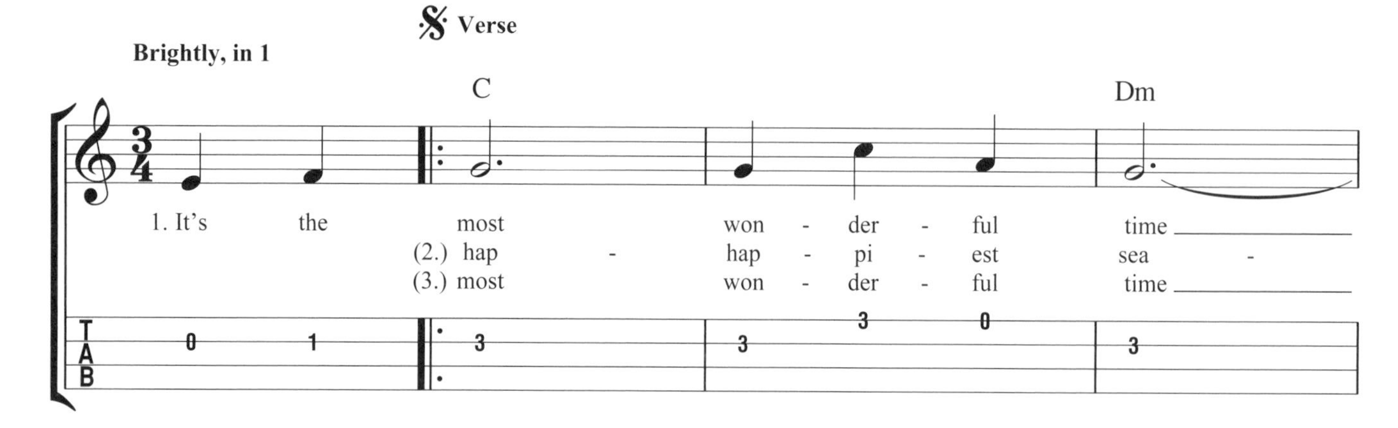

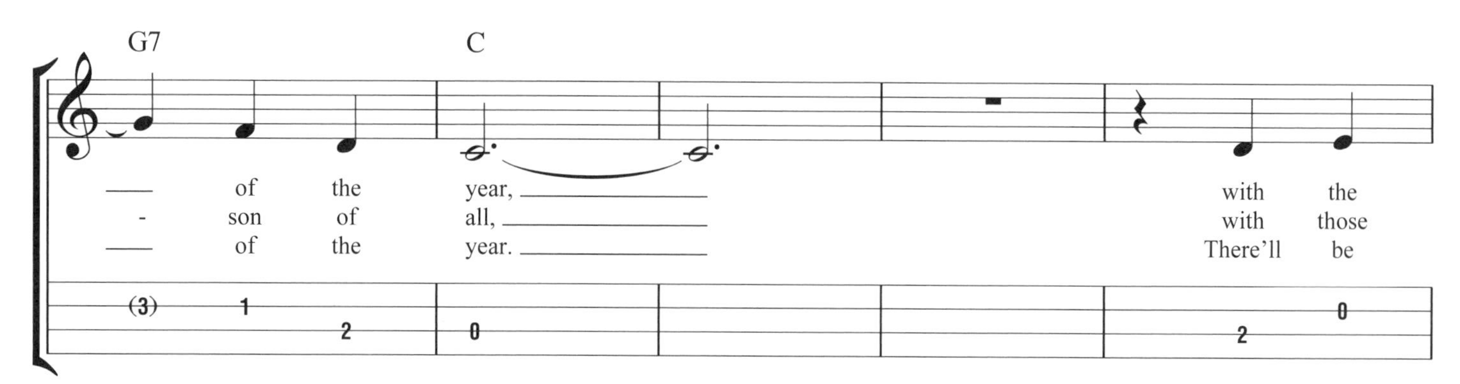

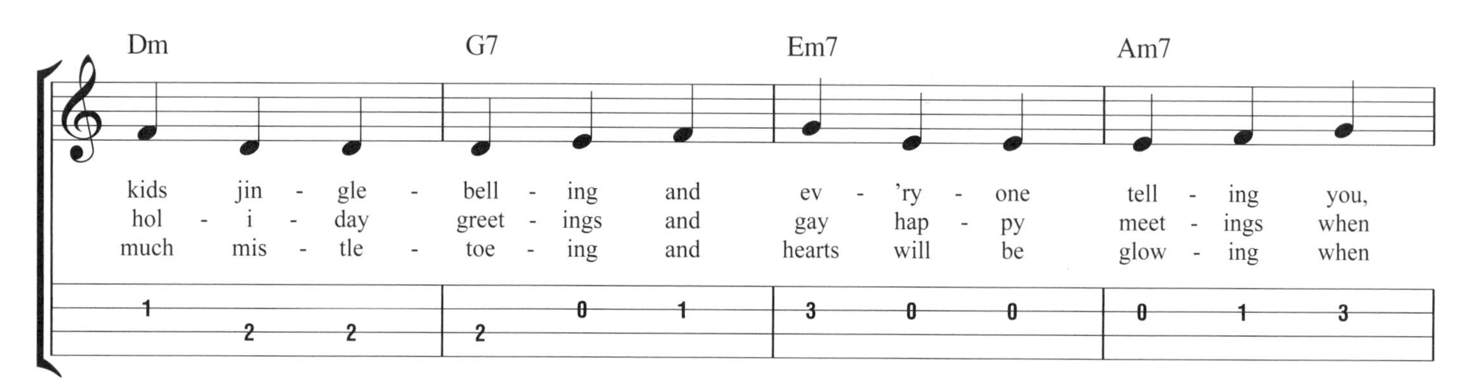

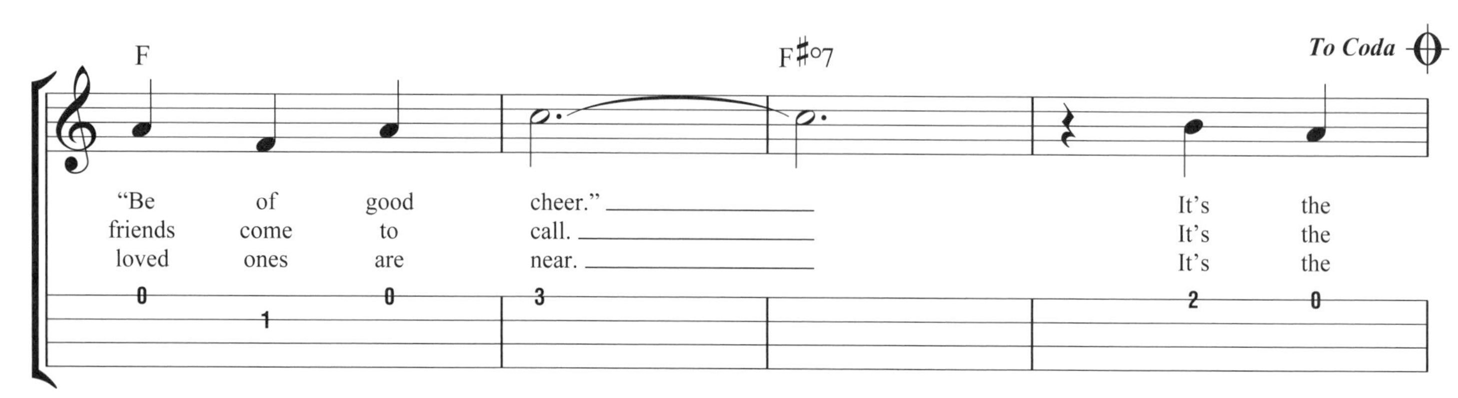

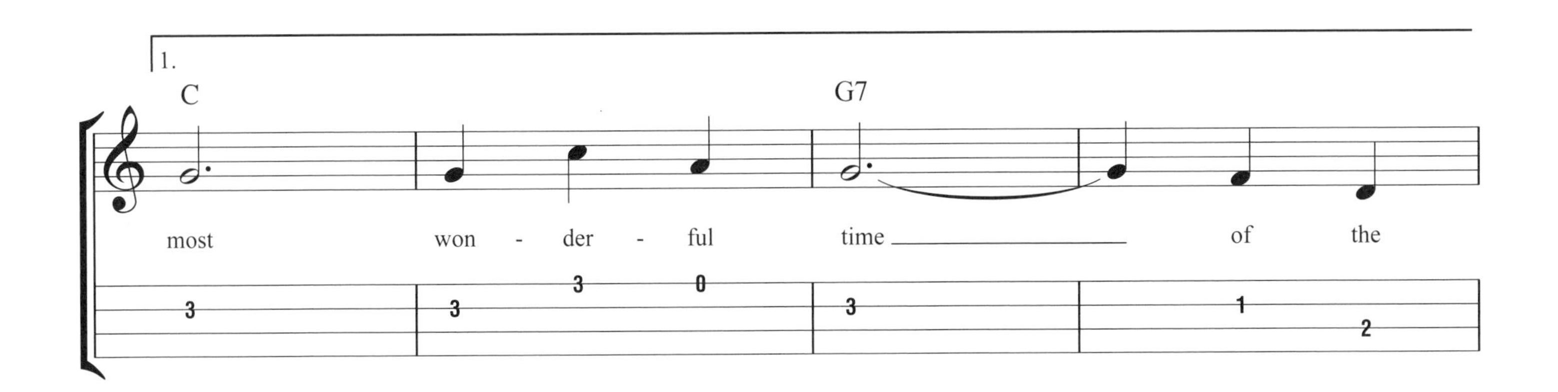
1.
C
G7
most won - der - ful time of the

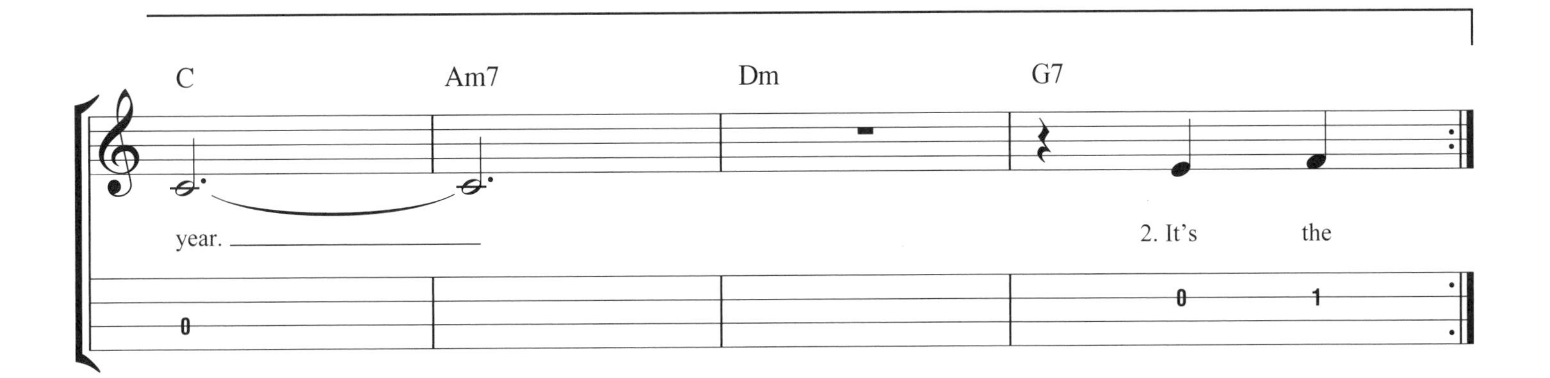
C
Am7
Dm
G7
year.
2. It's the

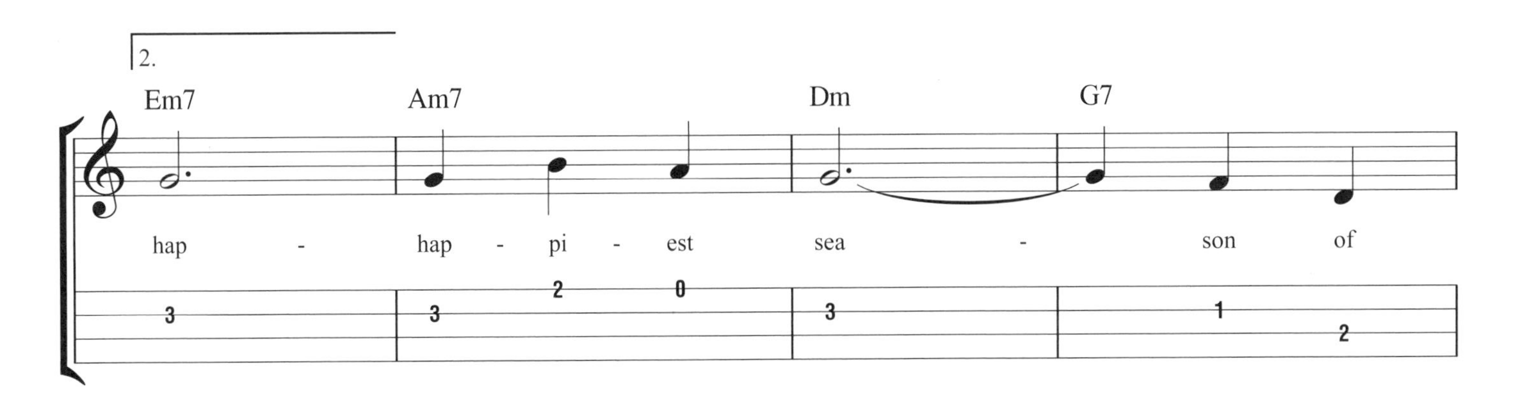
2.
Em7
Am7
Dm
G7
hap - hap - pi - est sea - son of

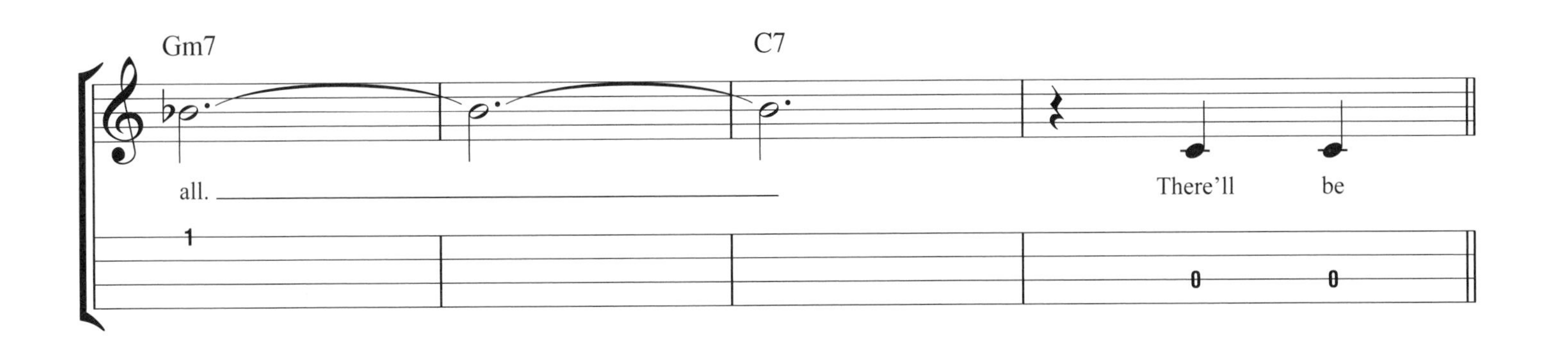
Gm7
C7
all.
There'll be

Bridge

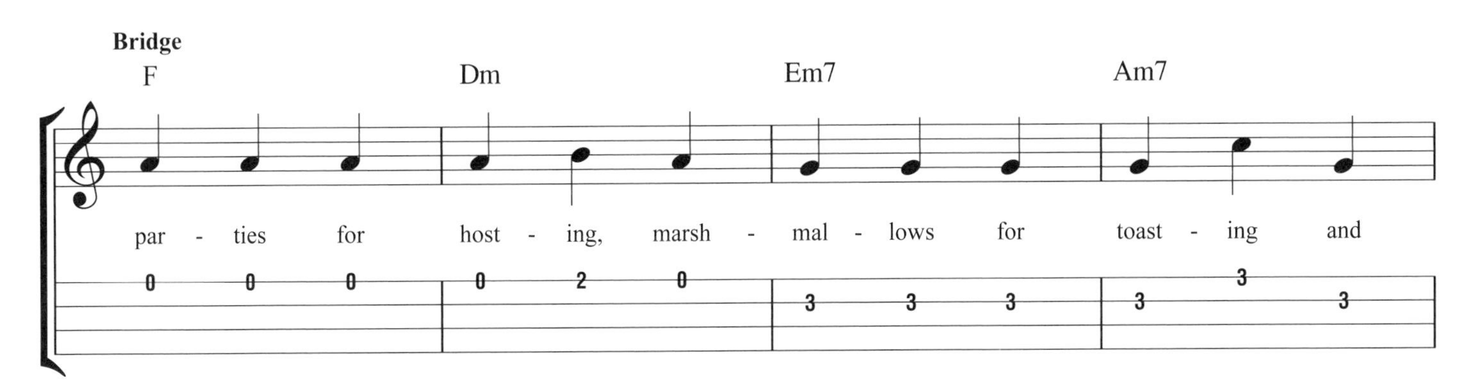
F
Dm
Em7
Am7
par - ties for host - ing, marsh - mal - lows for toast - ing and

Dm
G7
C
car - ol - ing out in the snow. There'll be

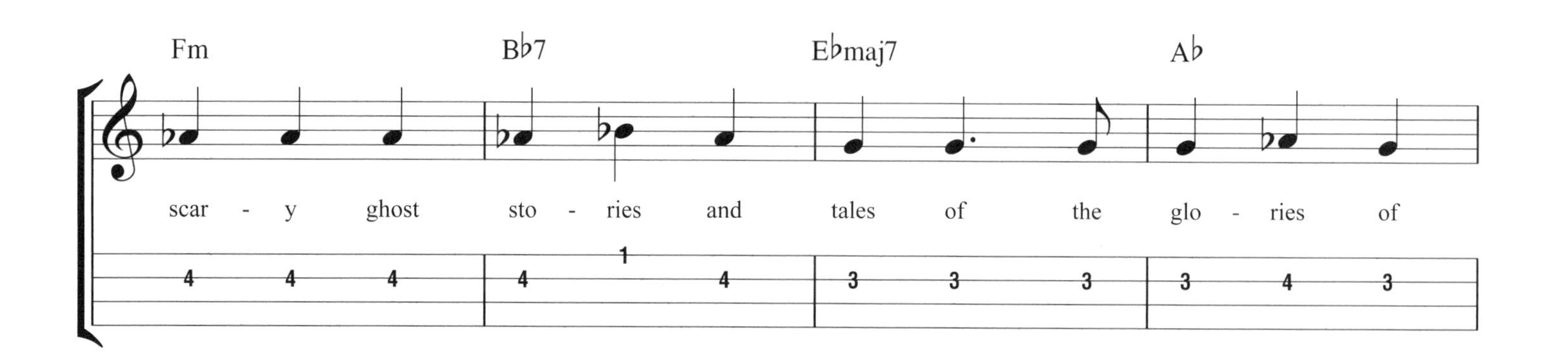
Fm
B♭7
E♭maj7
A♭
scar - y ghost sto - ries and tales of the glo - ries of

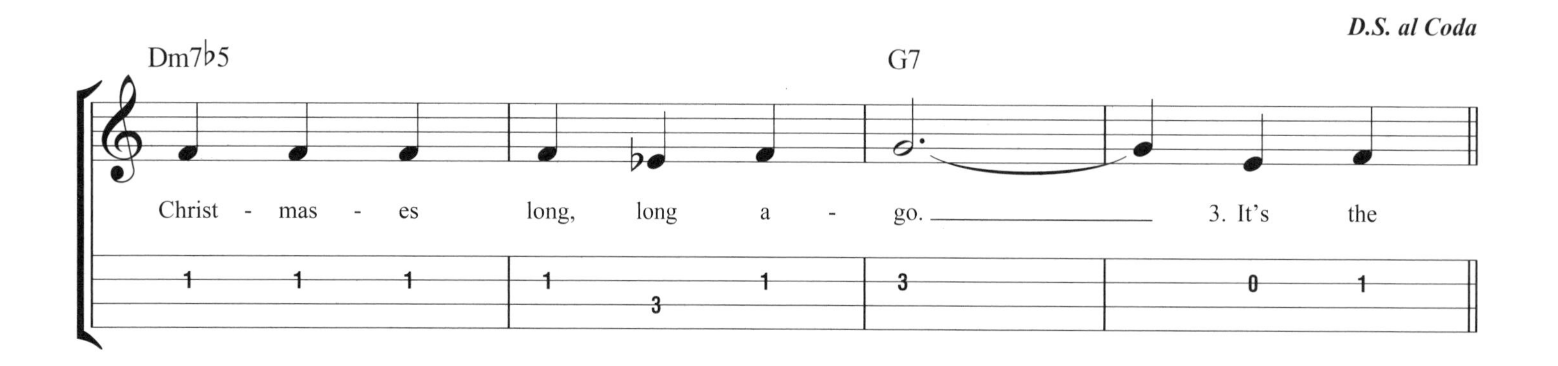
D.S. al Coda
Dm7♭5
G7
Christ - mas - es long, long a - go.
3. It's the

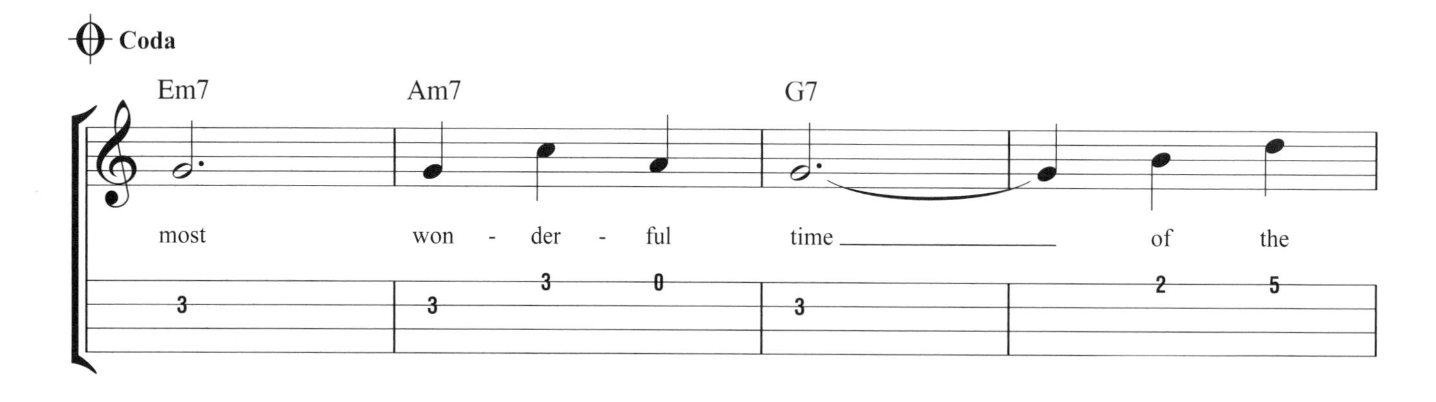
Coda
Em7
Am7
G7
most won - der - ful time of the

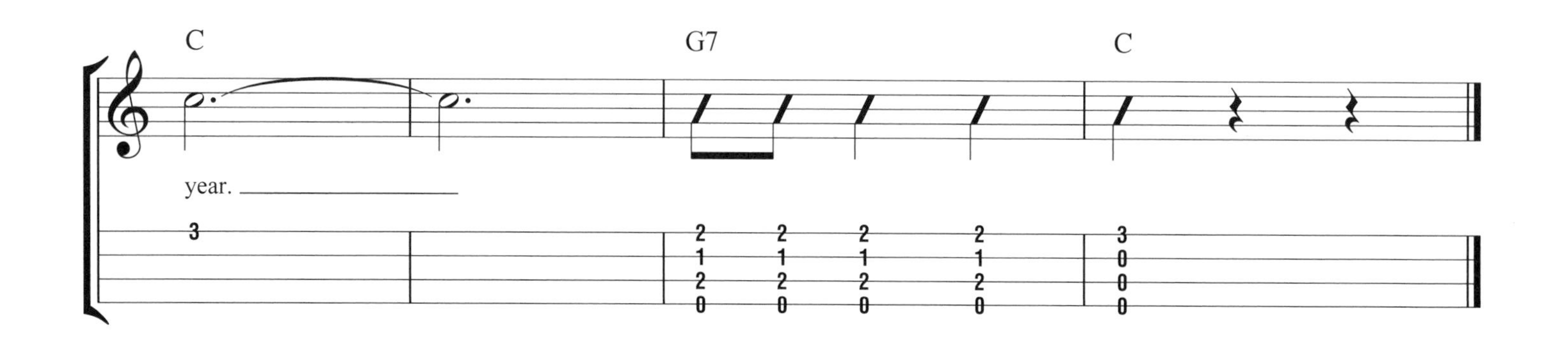
C
G7
C
year.

Merry Christmas, Darling

Words and Music by Richard Carpenter and Frank Pooler

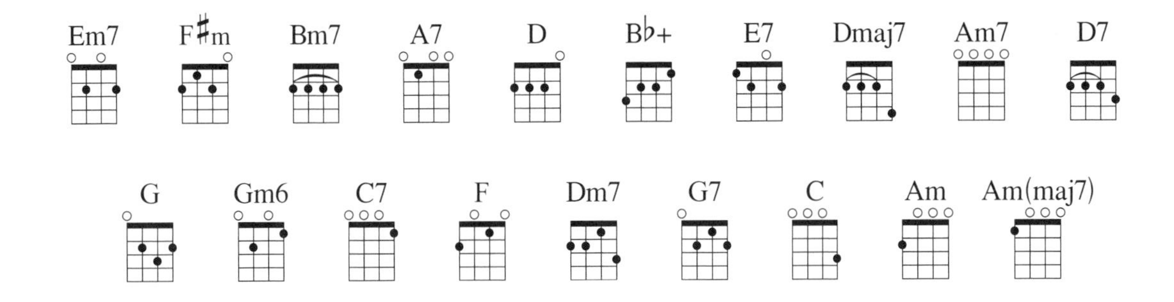

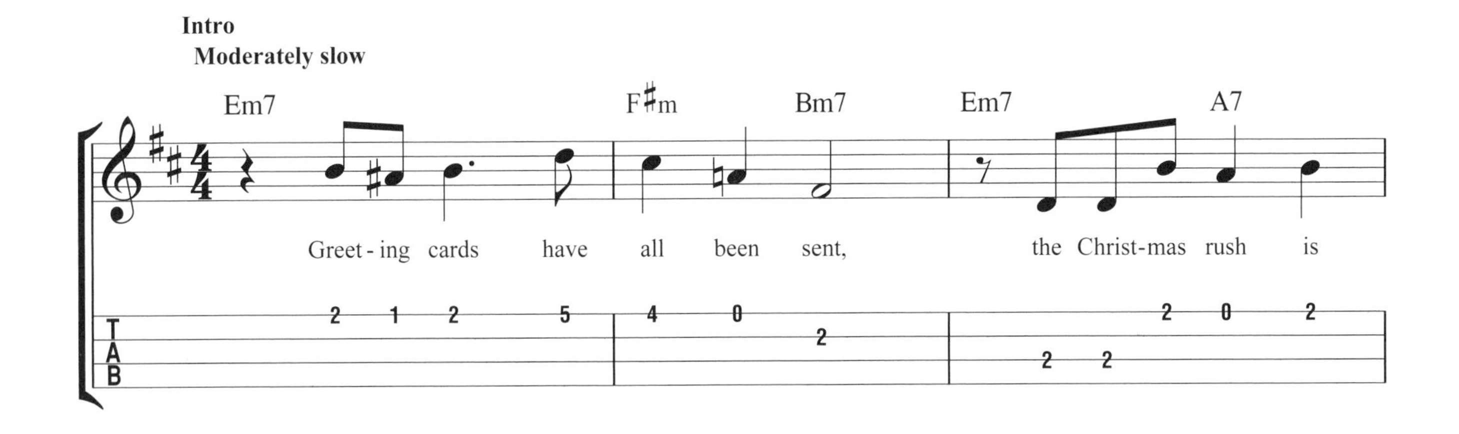

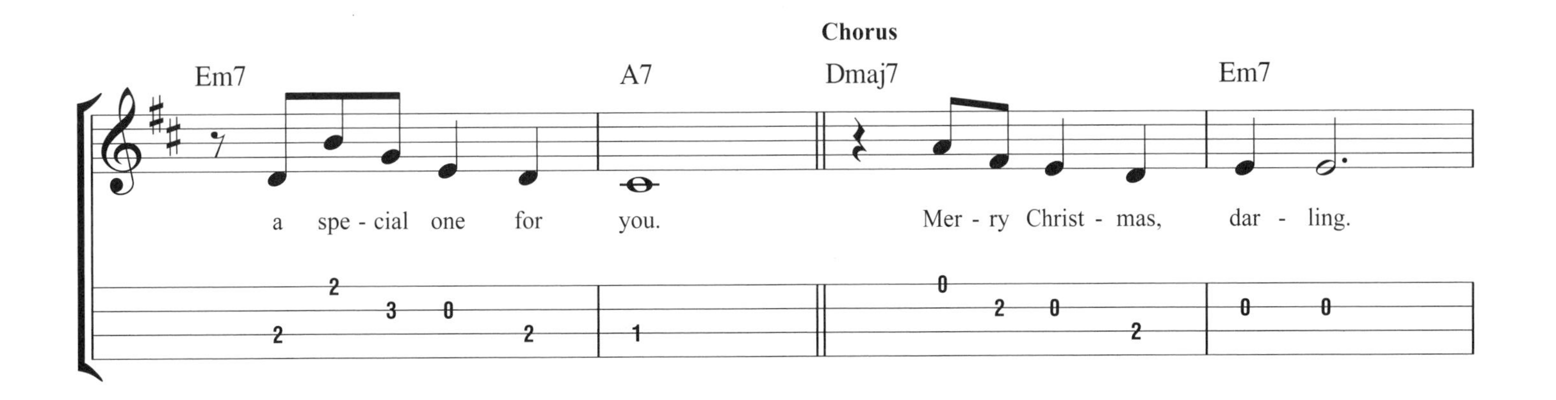

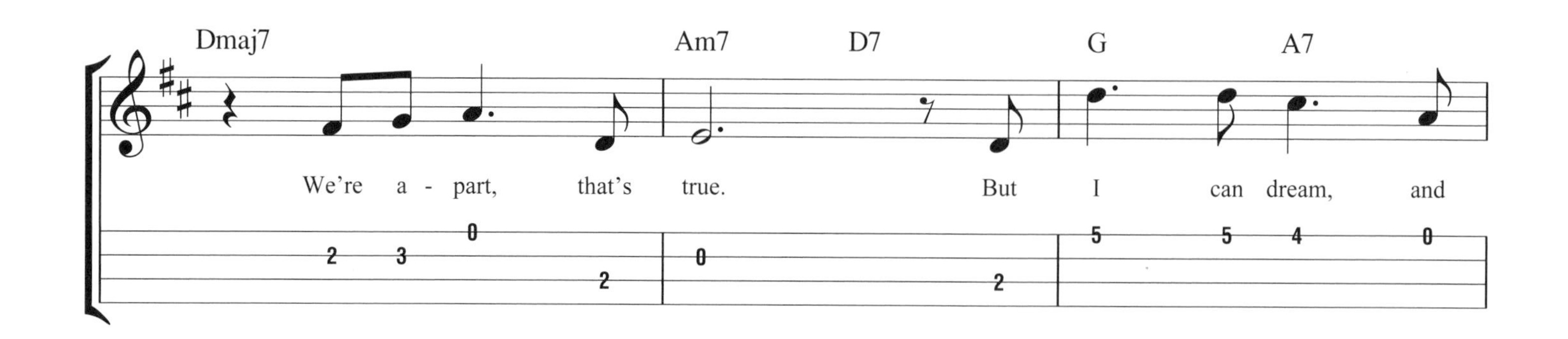
Dmaj7 Am7 D7 G A7
We're a - part, that's true. But I can dream, and

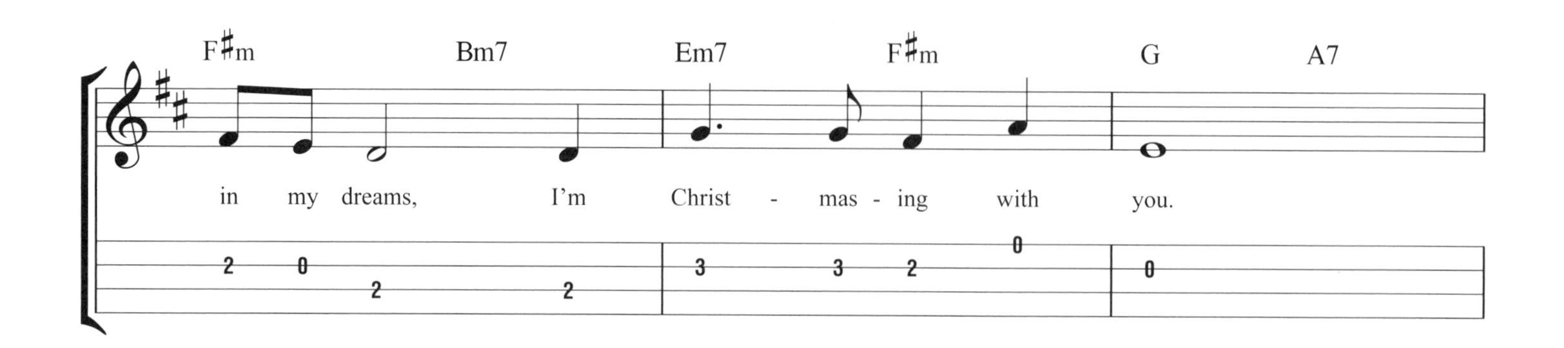
F♯m Bm7 Em7 F♯m G A7
in my dreams, I'm Christ - mas - ing with you.

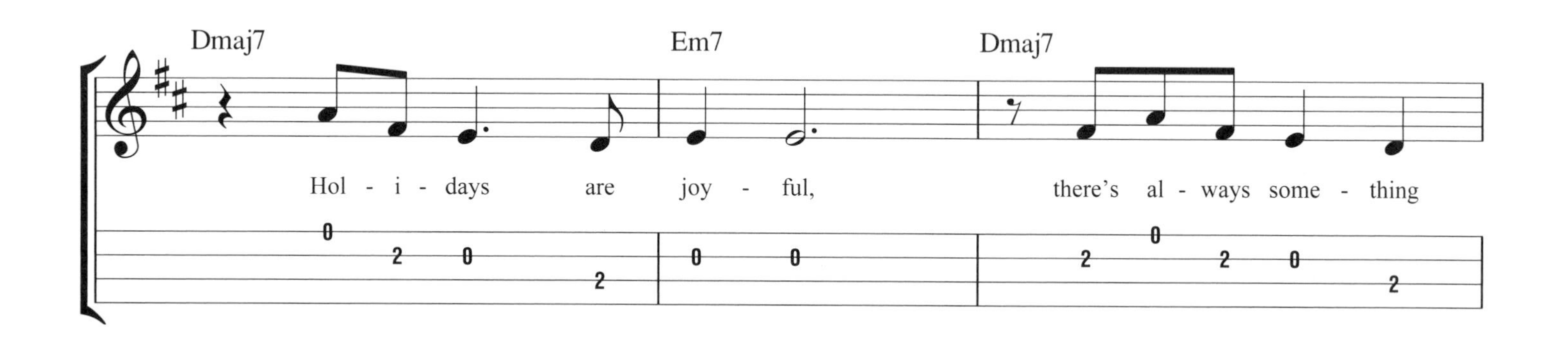
Dmaj7 Em7 Dmaj7
Hol - i - days are joy - ful, there's al - ways some - thing

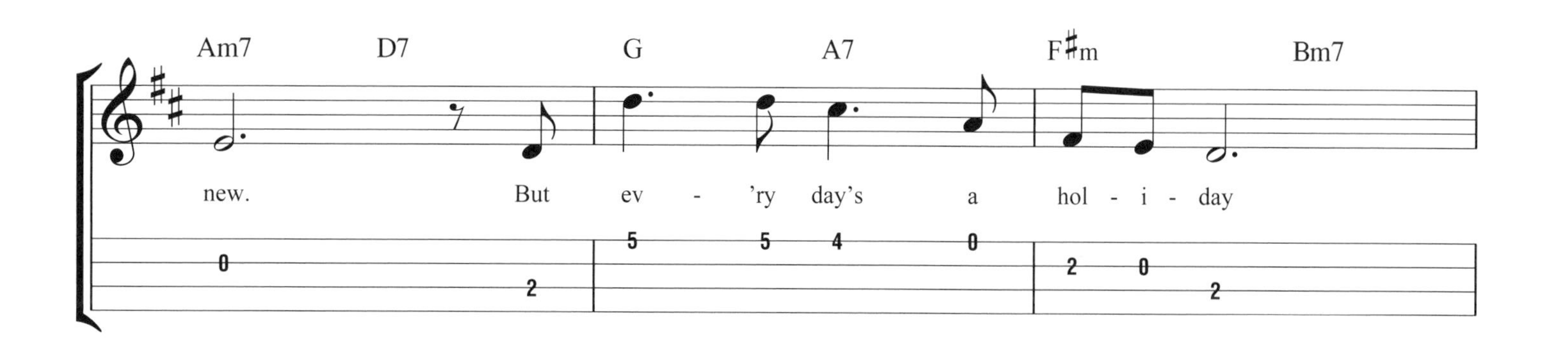
Am7 D7 G A7 F♯m Bm7
new. But ev - 'ry day's a hol - i - day

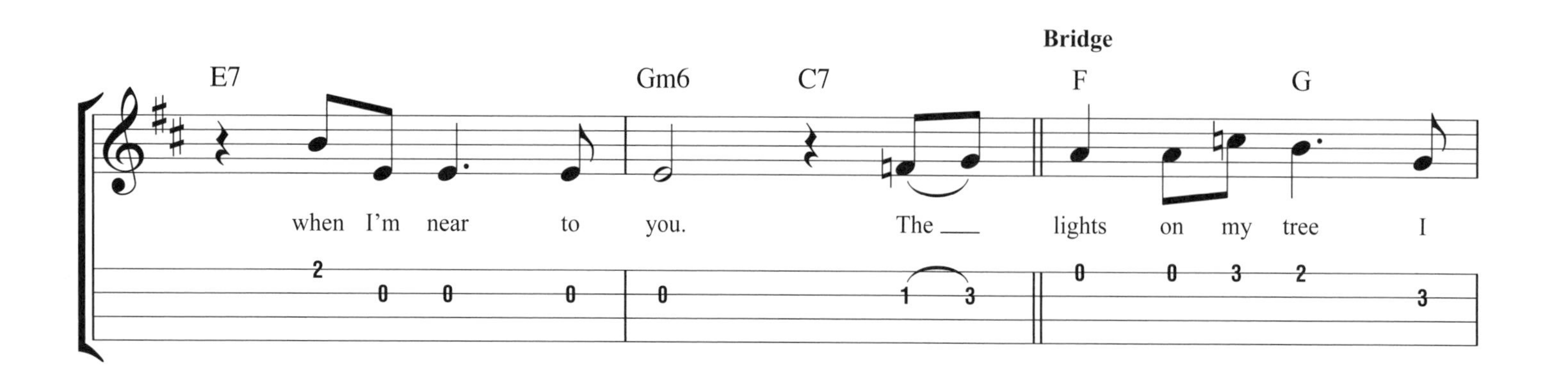
Bridge
E7 Gm6 C7 F G
when I'm near to you. The lights on my tree I

Em7 Am7 Dm7 G7 C
wish you could see, I wish it ev - 'ry day. The

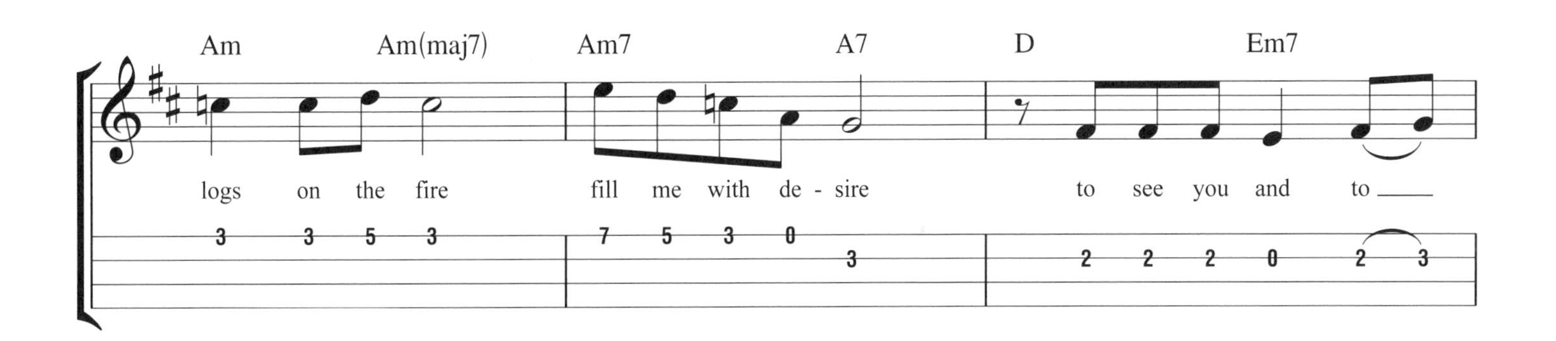
Am Am(maj7) Am7 A7 D Em7
logs on the fire fill me with de - sire to see you and to

Outro-Chorus
F♯m Em7 A7 Dmaj7 Em7
say that I wish you Mer - ry Christ - mas,

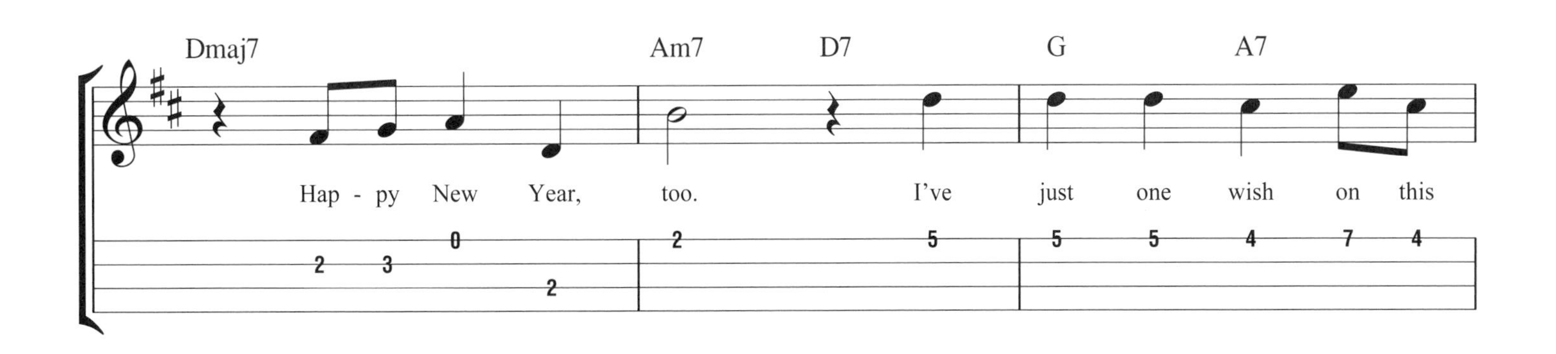
Dmaj7 Am7 D7 G A7
Hap - py New Year, too. I've just one wish on this

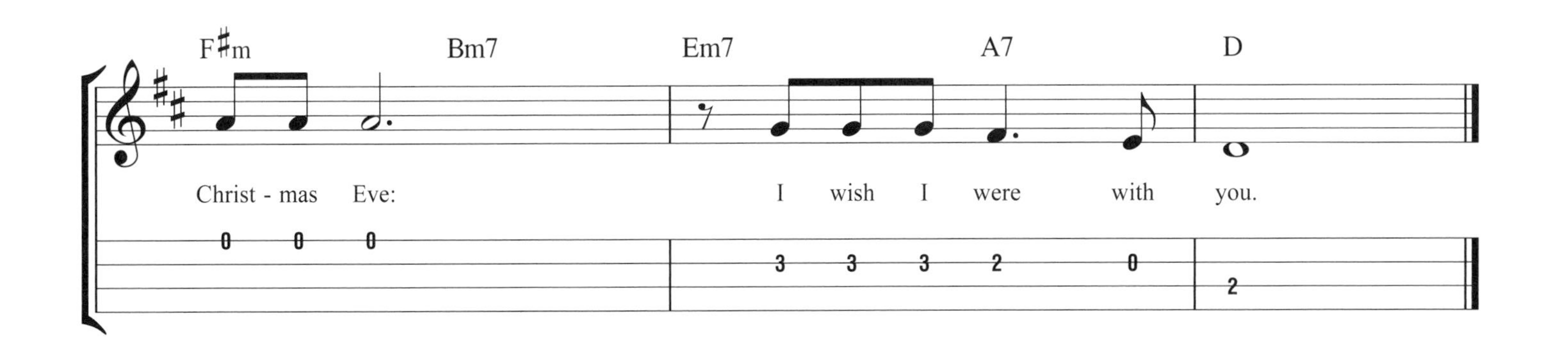
F♯m Bm7 Em7 A7 D
Christ - mas Eve: I wish I were with you.

Rudolph the Red-Nosed Reindeer

Music and Lyrics by Johnny Marks

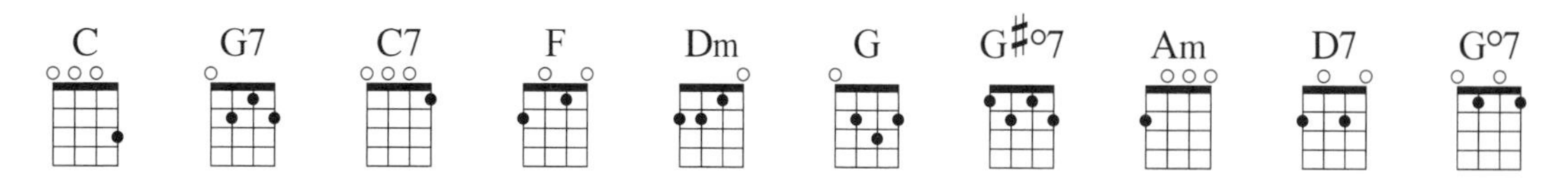

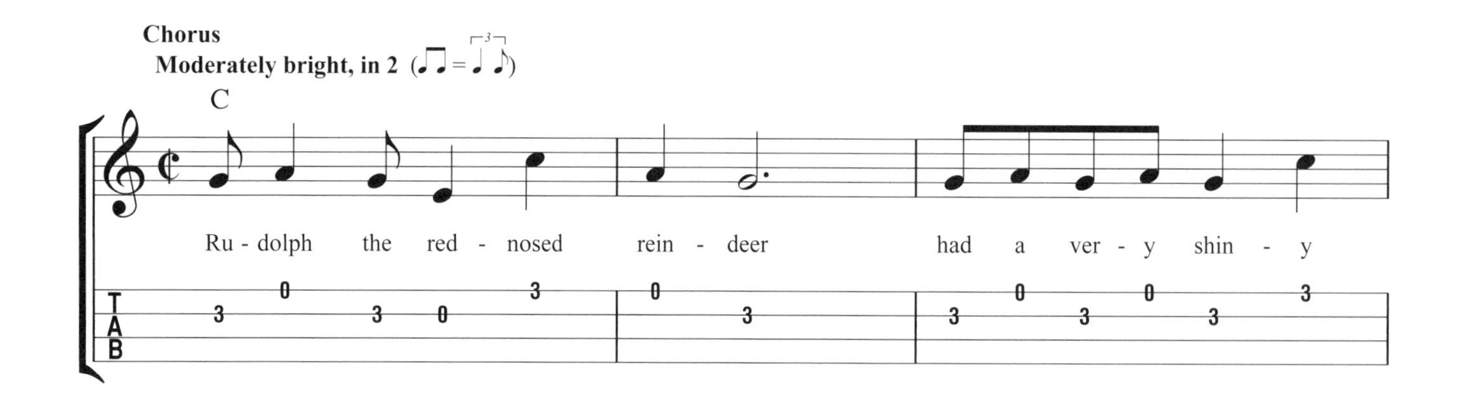

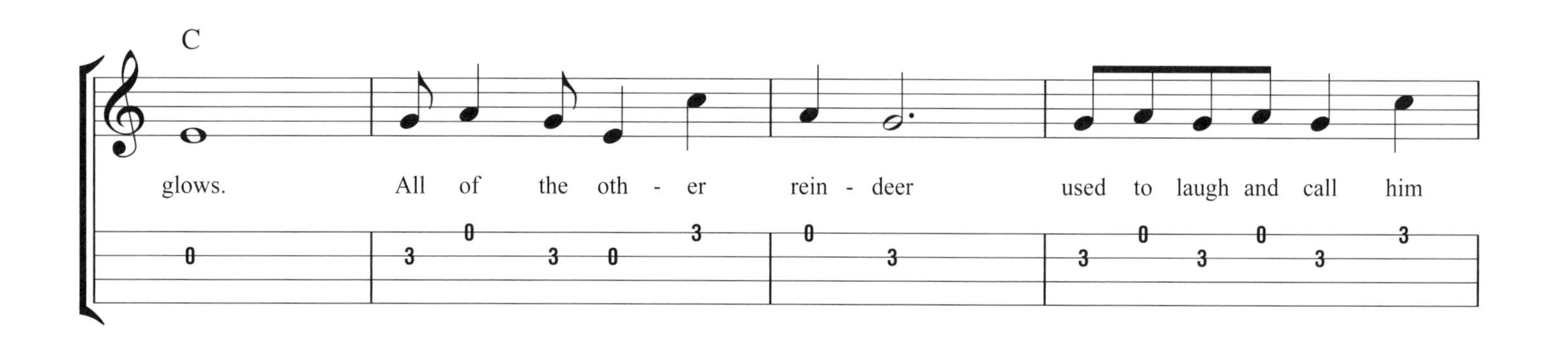

Bridge
C C7 F C Dm G7
games. Then one fog - gy Christ - mas Eve, San - ta came to

C G G♯°7 Am D7
say, "Ru - dolph, with your nose so bright, won't you guide my

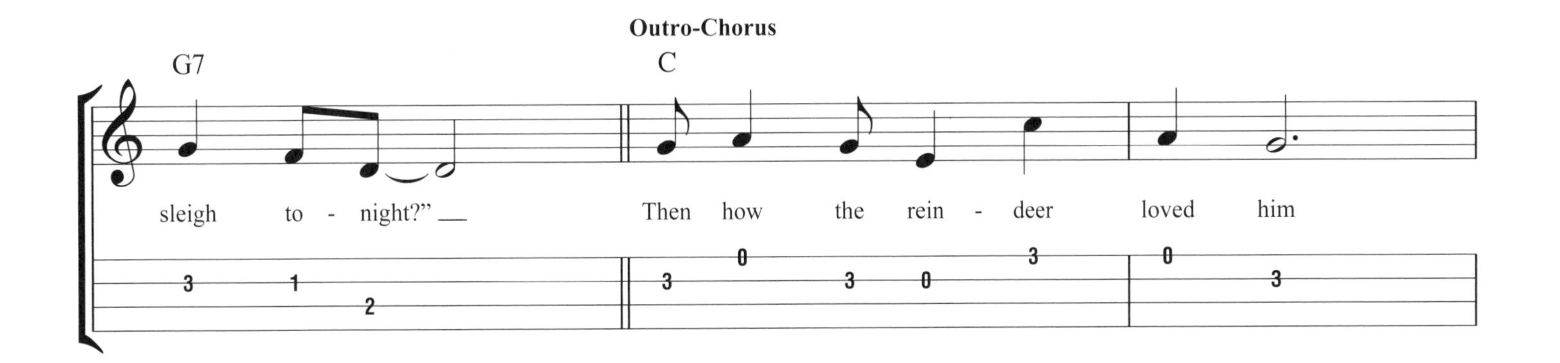
Outro-Chorus
G7 C
sleigh to - night?" Then how the rein - deer loved him

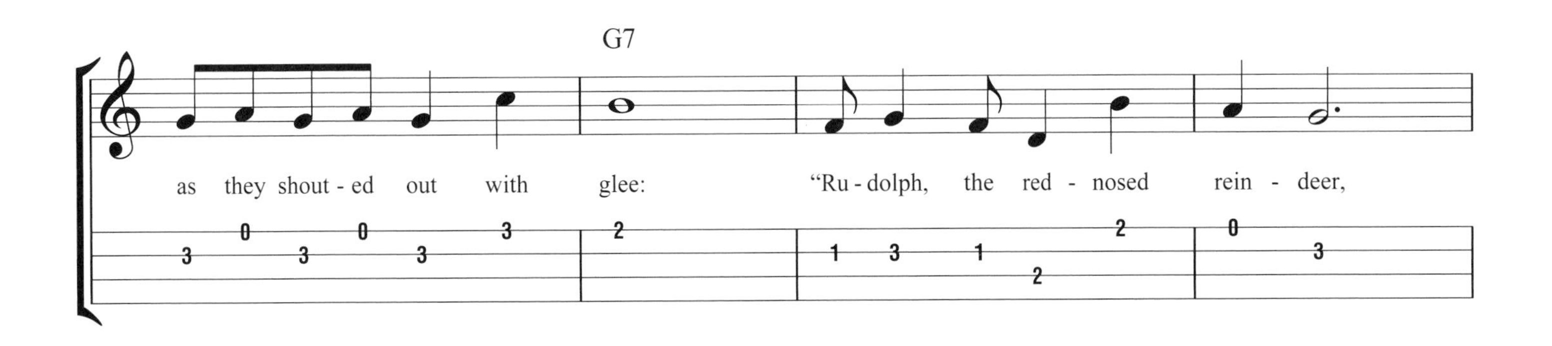
G7
as they shout - ed out with glee: "Ru - dolph, the red - nosed rein - deer,

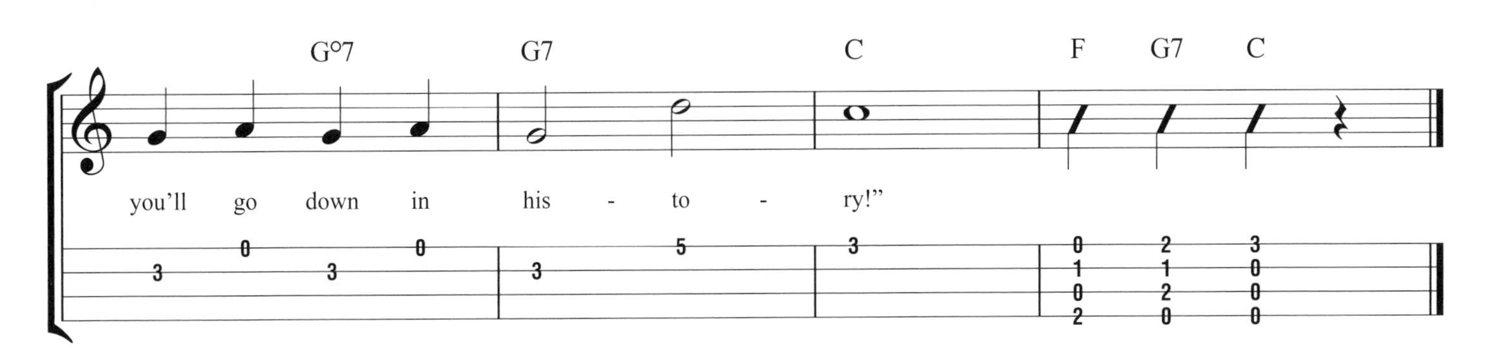
G°7 G7 C F G7 C
you'll go down in his - to - ry!"

Santa Claus Is Comin' to Town

Words by Haven Gillespie
Music by J. Fred Coots

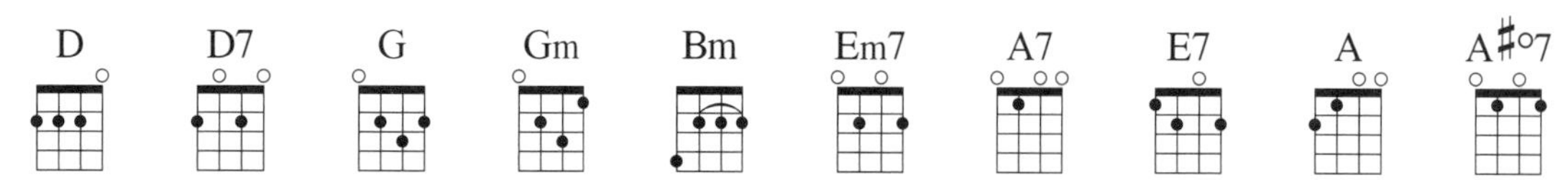

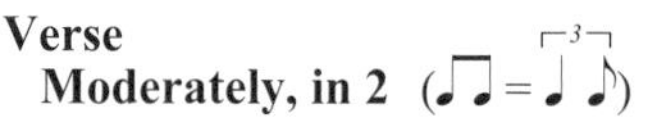

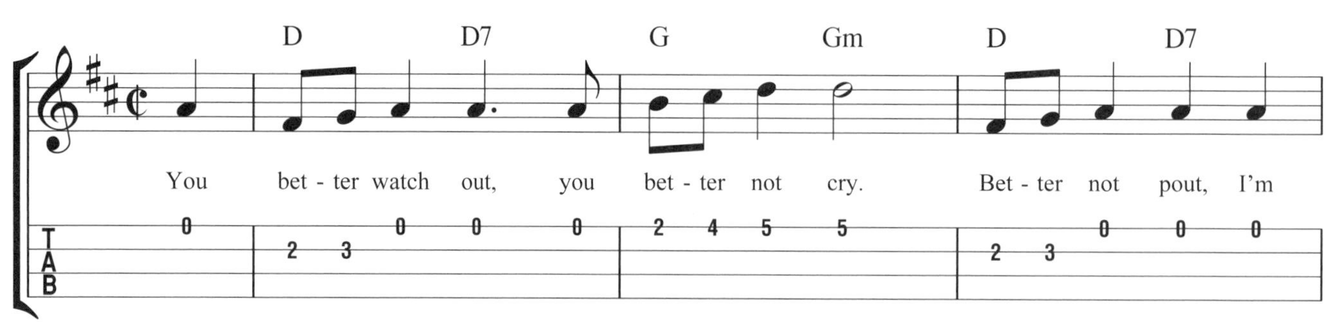

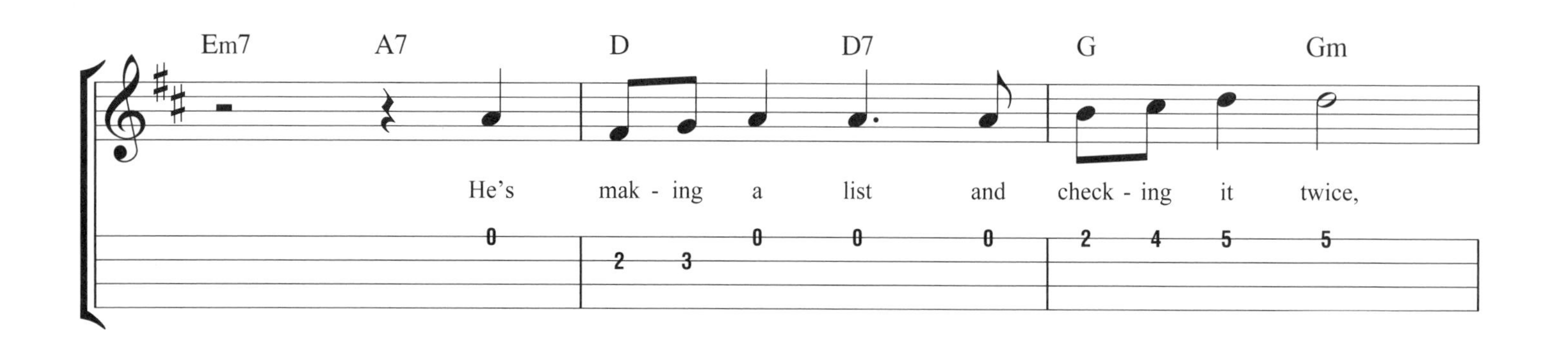

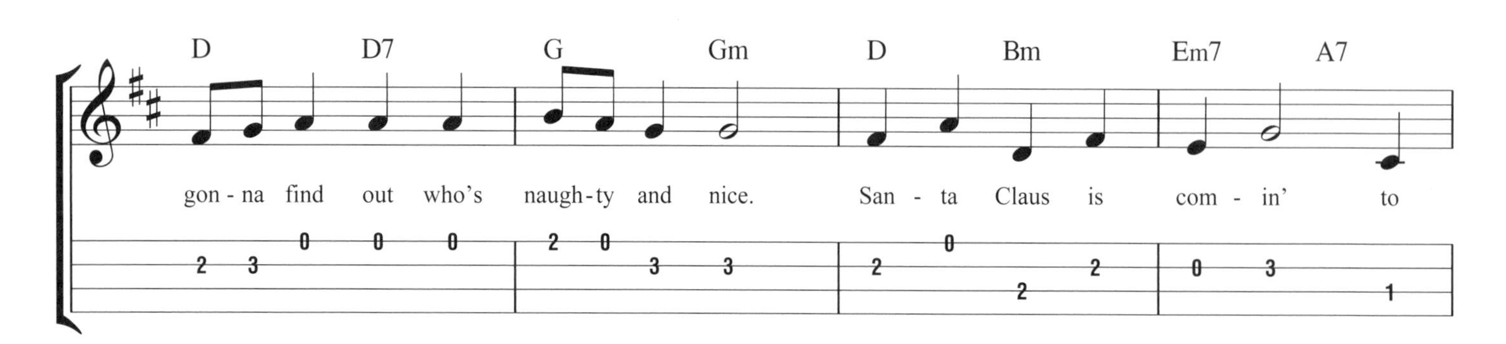

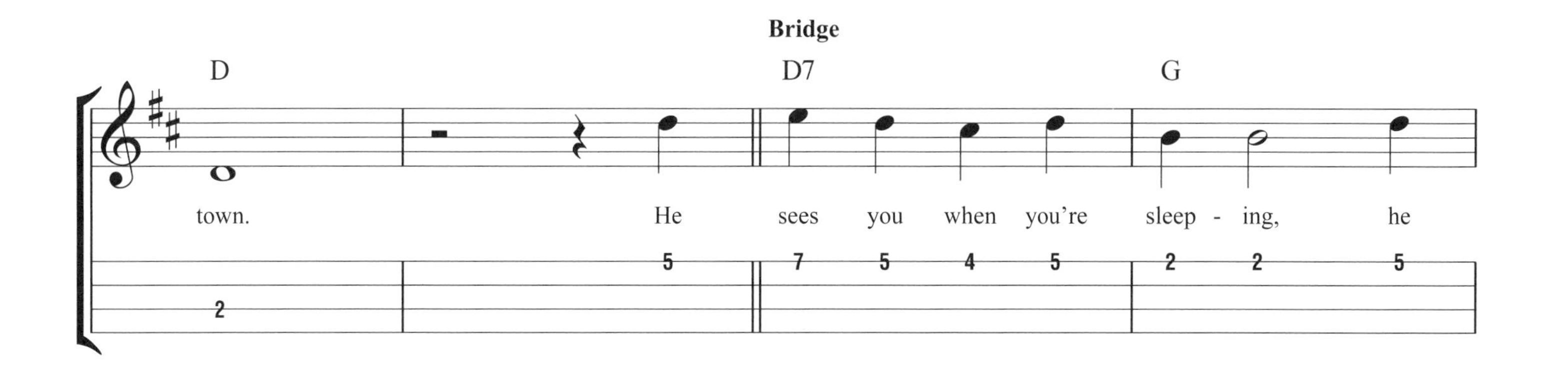
Bridge
D
D7
G
town.
He
sees
you
when
you're
sleep - ing,
he
2
5
7 5 4 5
2 2 5

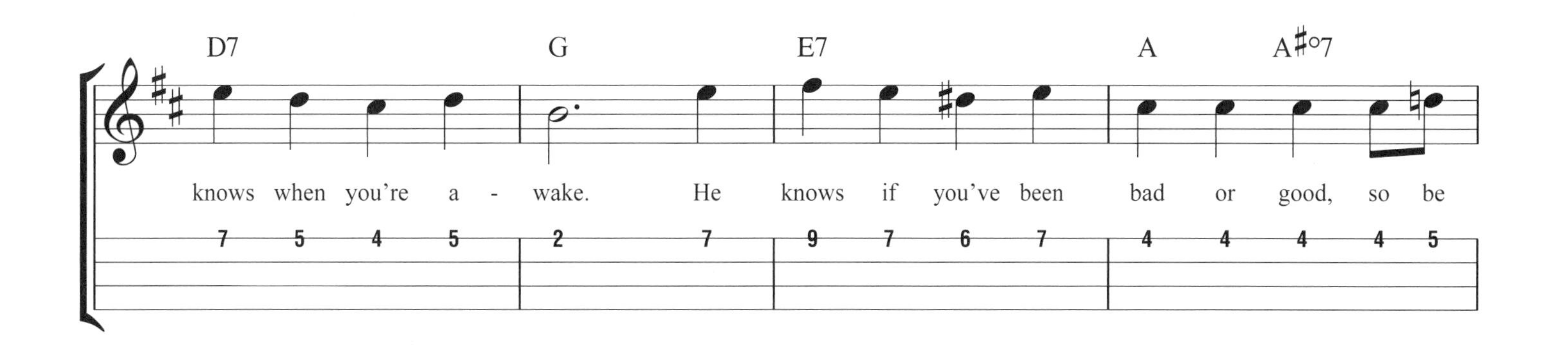
D7
G
E7
A
A♯°7
knows when you're a - wake.
He
knows
if
you've been
bad or good, so be
7 5 4 5
2 7
9 7 6 7
4 4 4 4 5

Outro-Verse
Bm
E7
A7
D
D7
G
Gm
good for good - ness' sake!
Oh, you
bet - ter watch out, you
bet - ter not cry.
7 5 4 2
0 0 0
2 3 0 0 0
2 4 5 5

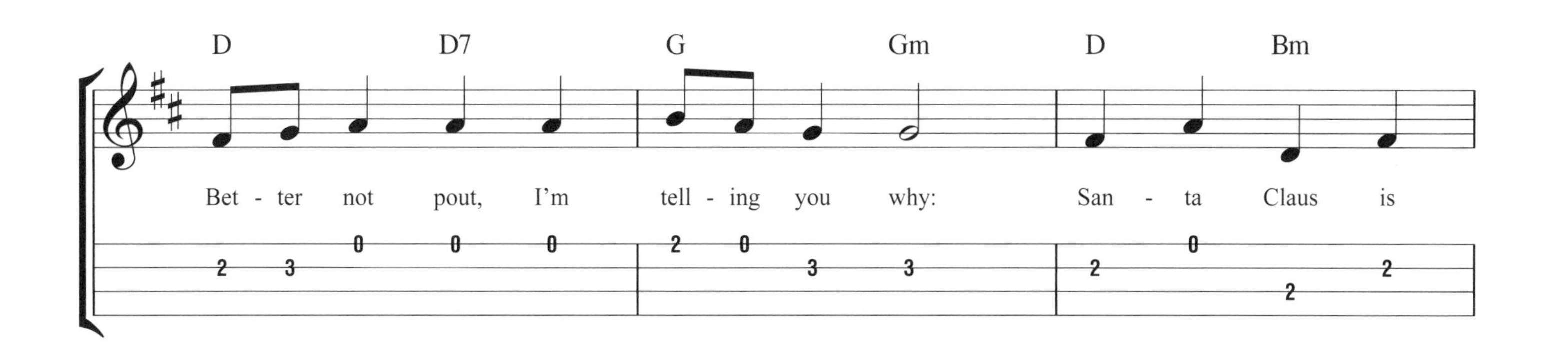
D
D7
G
Gm
D
Bm
Bet - ter not pout, I'm
tell - ing you why:
San - ta Claus is
2 3 0 0 0
2 0 3 3
2 0 2 2

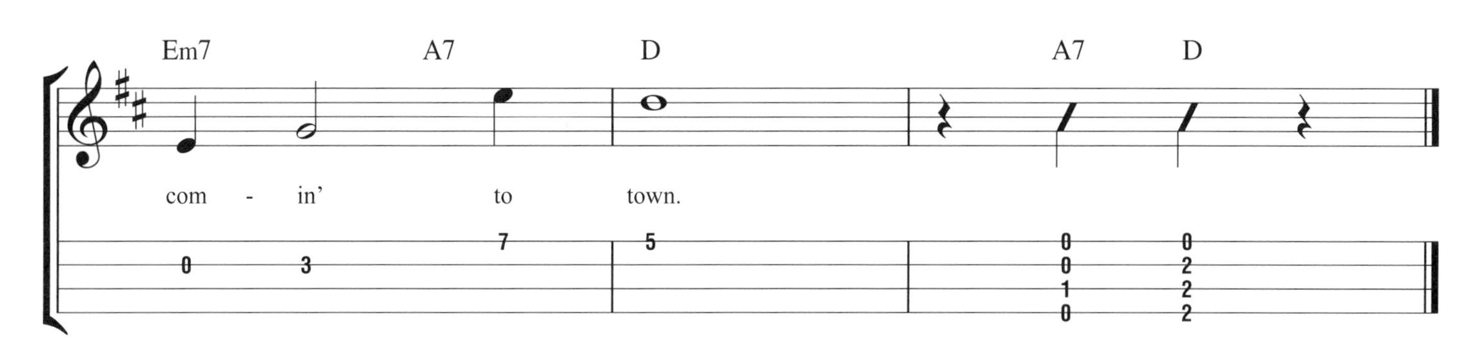
Em7
A7
D
A7
D
com - in' to
town.
0 3 7
5
0 0 1 0
0 2 2 2

Silver Bells

from the Paramount Picture THE LEMON DROP KID

Words and Music by Jay Livingston and Ray Evans

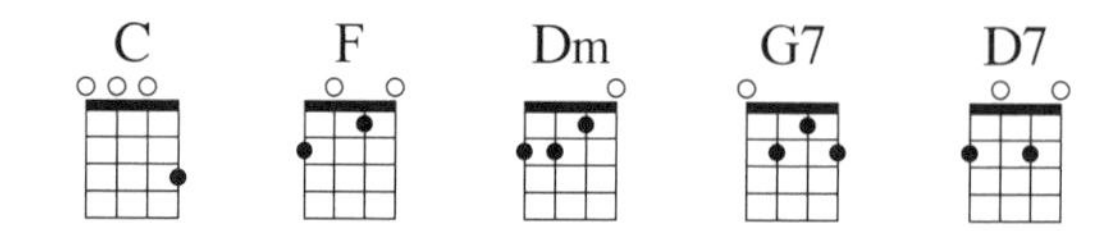

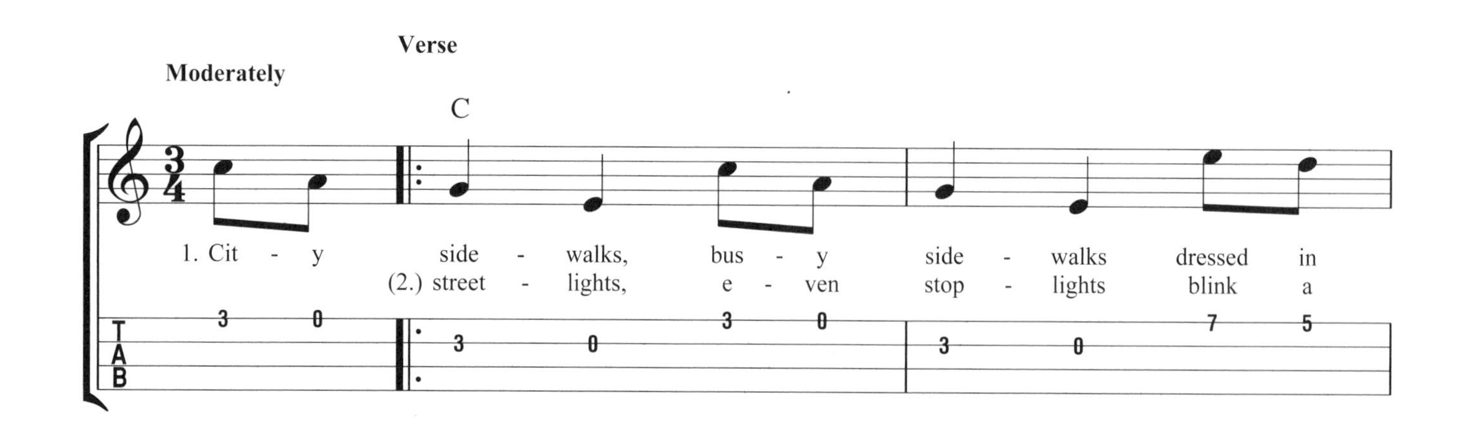

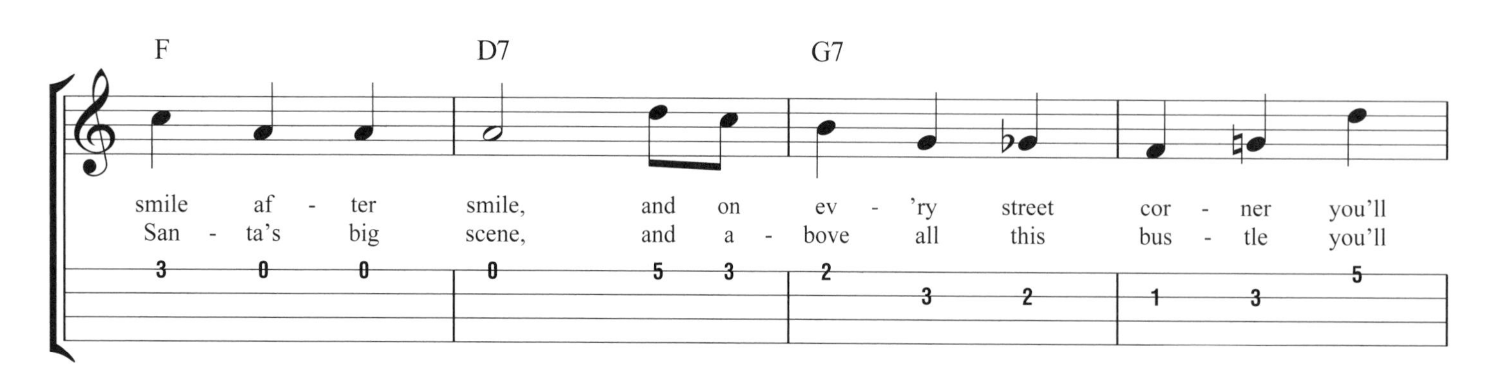

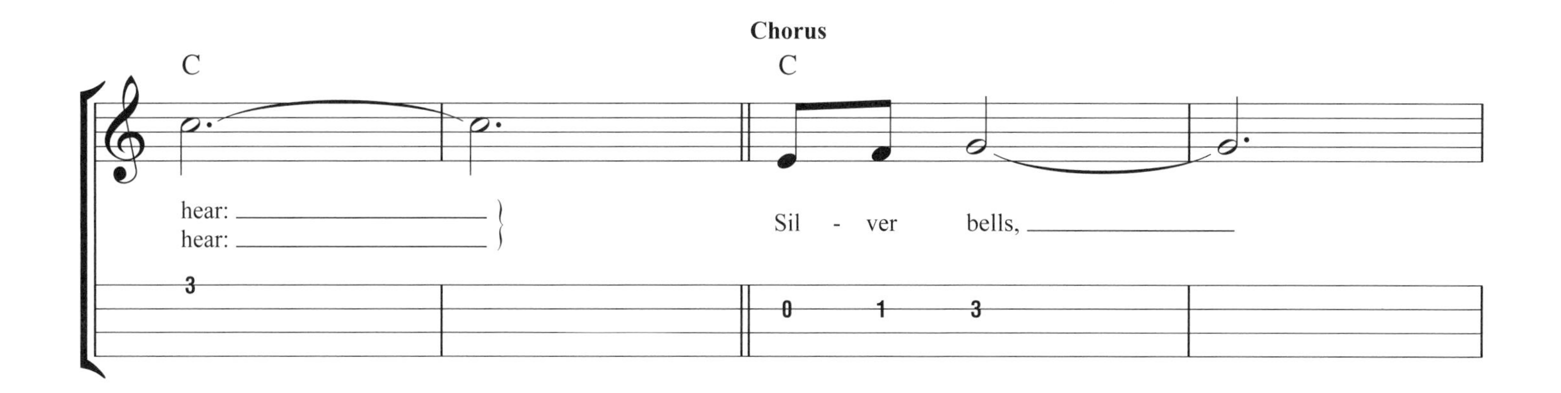
Chorus
C
C
hear:
hear:
Sil - ver bells,
0 1 3

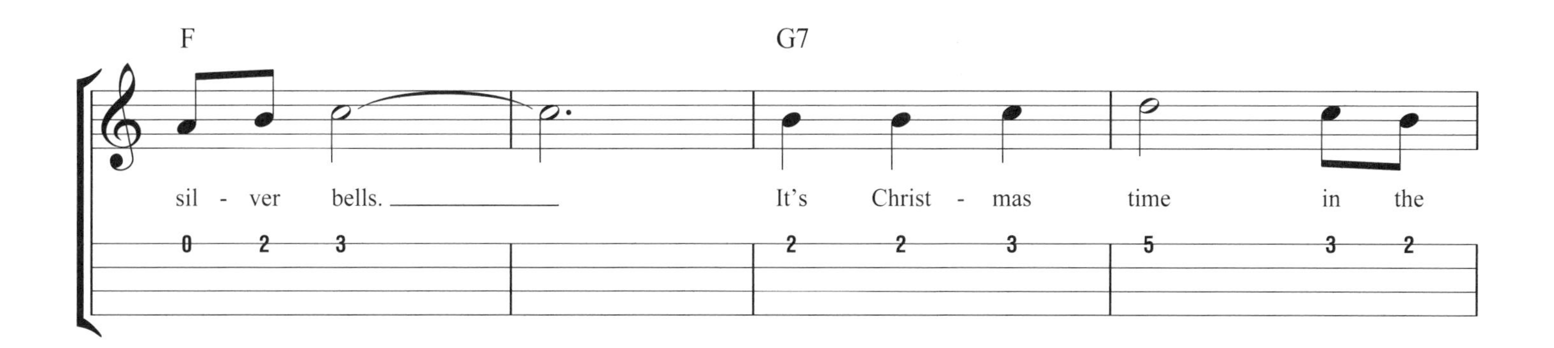
F
G7
sil - ver bells.
It's Christ - mas time in the
0 2 3
2 2 3 5 3 2

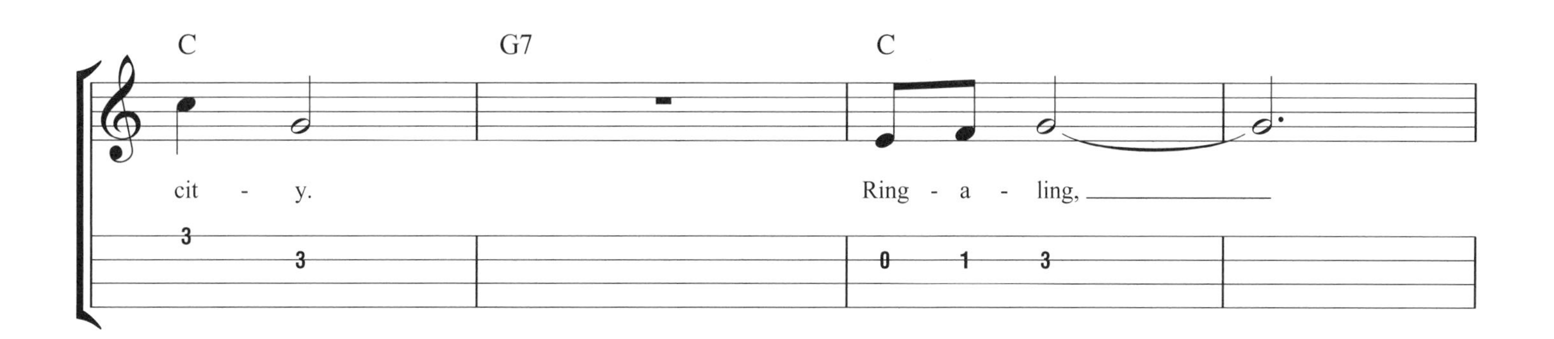
C
G7
C
cit - y.
Ring - a - ling,
0 1 3

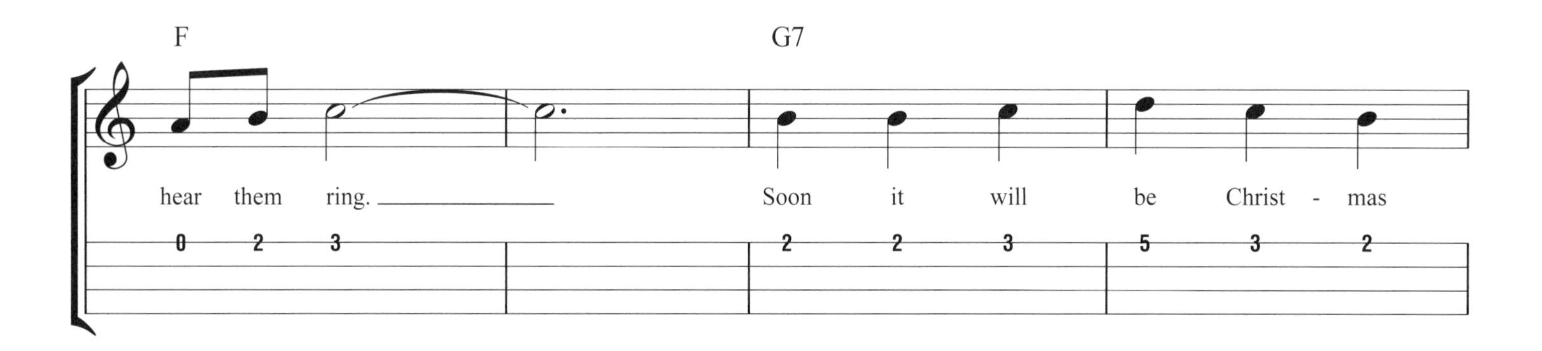
F
G7
hear them ring.
Soon it will be Christ - mas
0 2 3
2 2 3 5 3 2

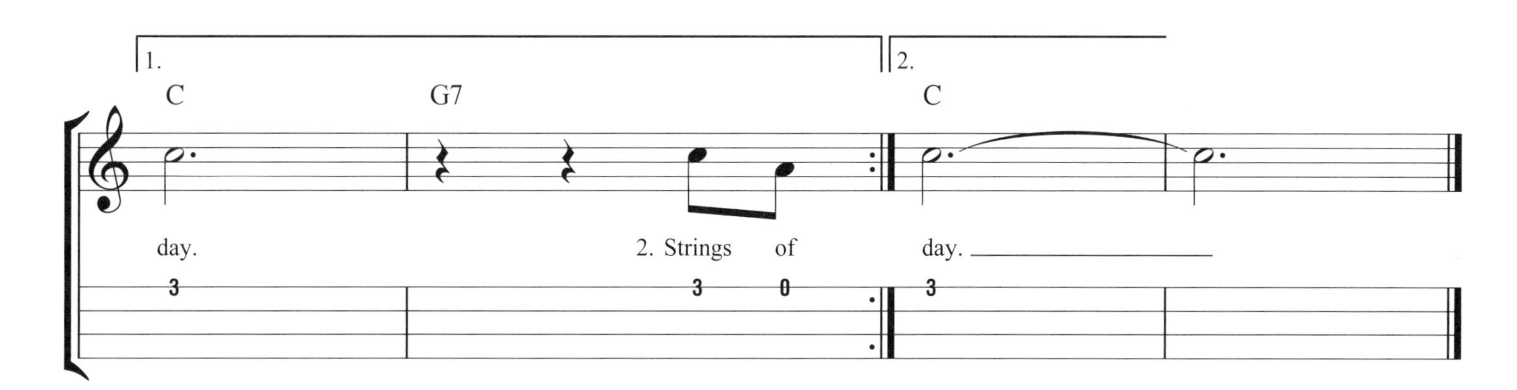
1.
2.
C
G7
C
day.
2. Strings of
day.
3 0

Somewhere in My Memory

from the Twentieth Century Fox Motion Picture HOME ALONE

Words by Leslie Bricusse
Music by John Williams

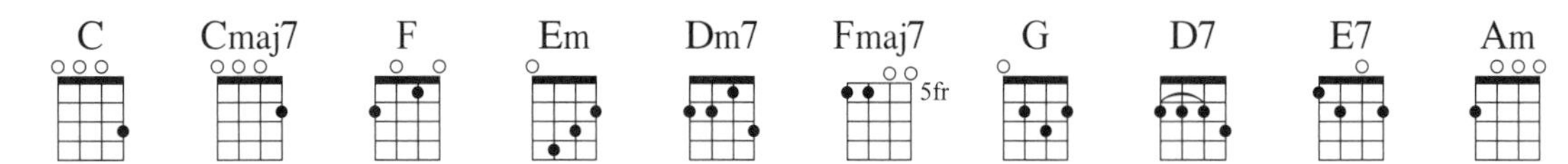

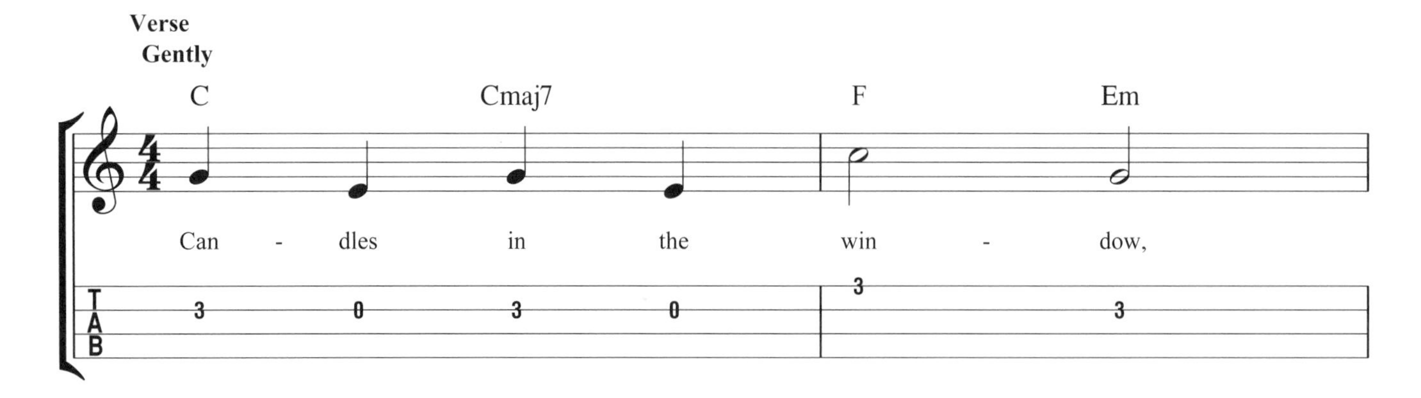

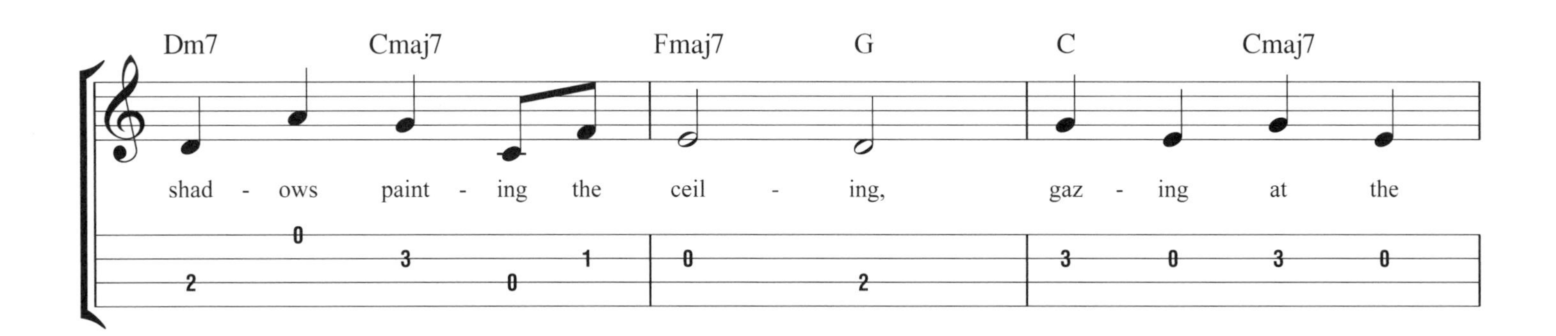

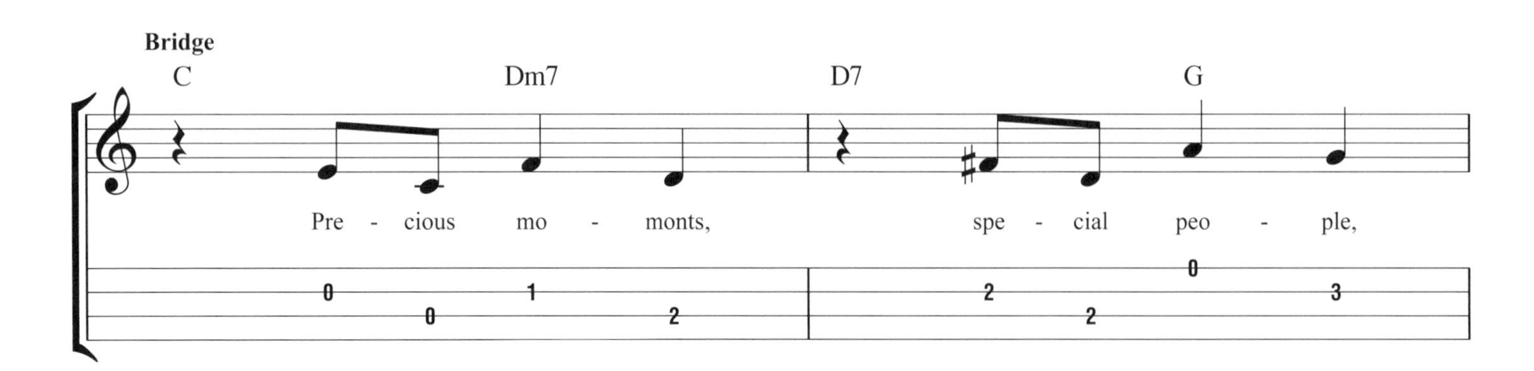

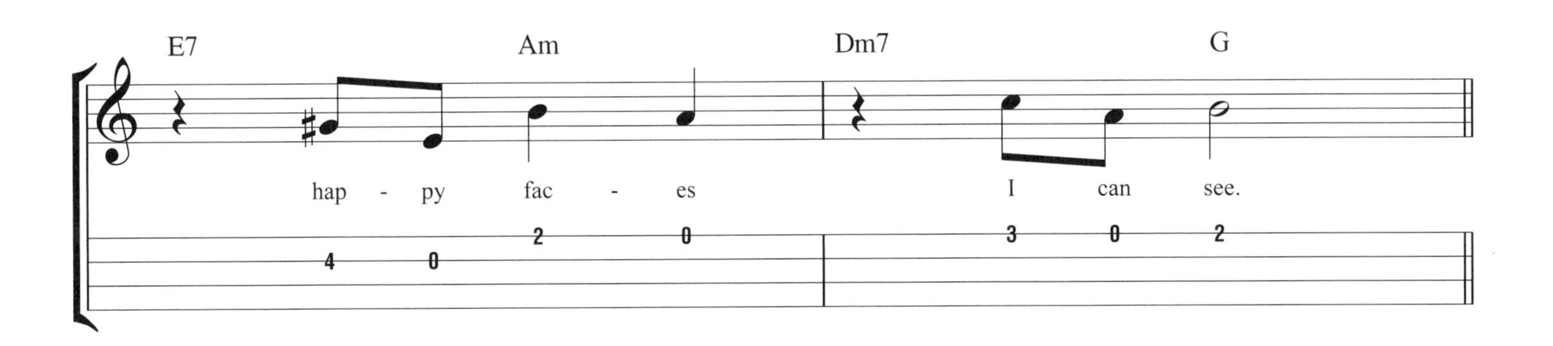
E7 Am Dm7 G
hap - py fac - es I can see.

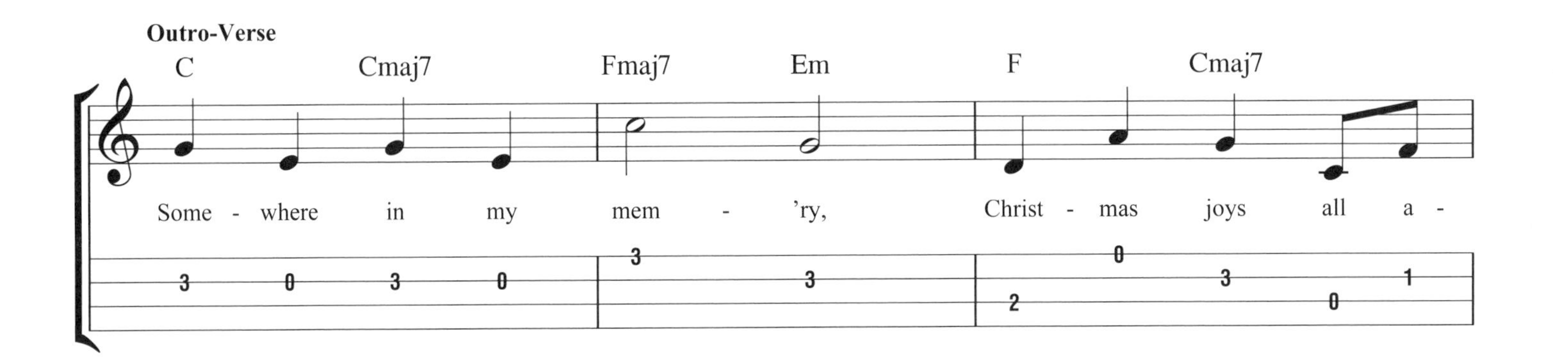
Outro-Verse
C Cmaj7 Fmaj7 Em F Cmaj7
Some - where in my mem - 'ry, Christ - mas joys all a -

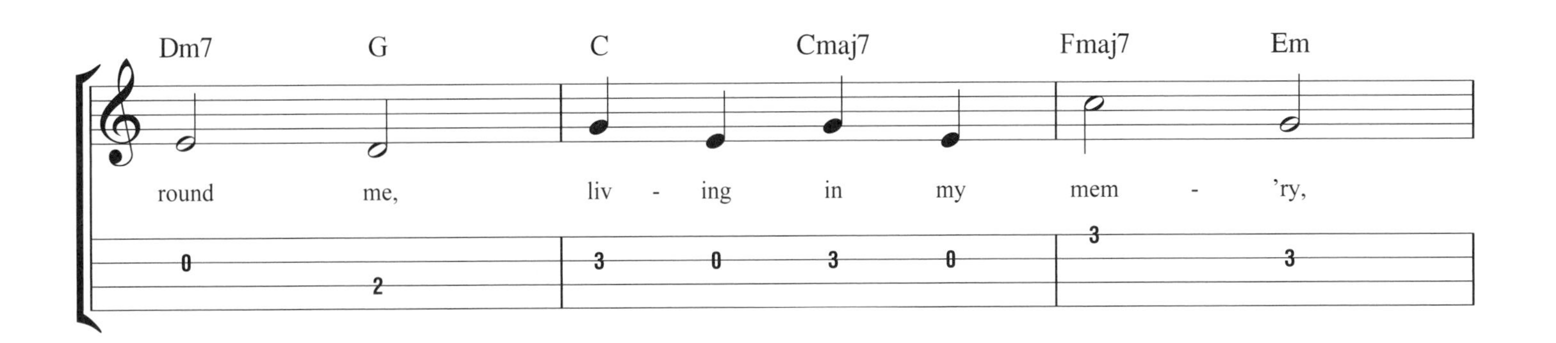
Dm7 G C Cmaj7 Fmaj7 Em
round me, liv - ing in my mem - 'ry,

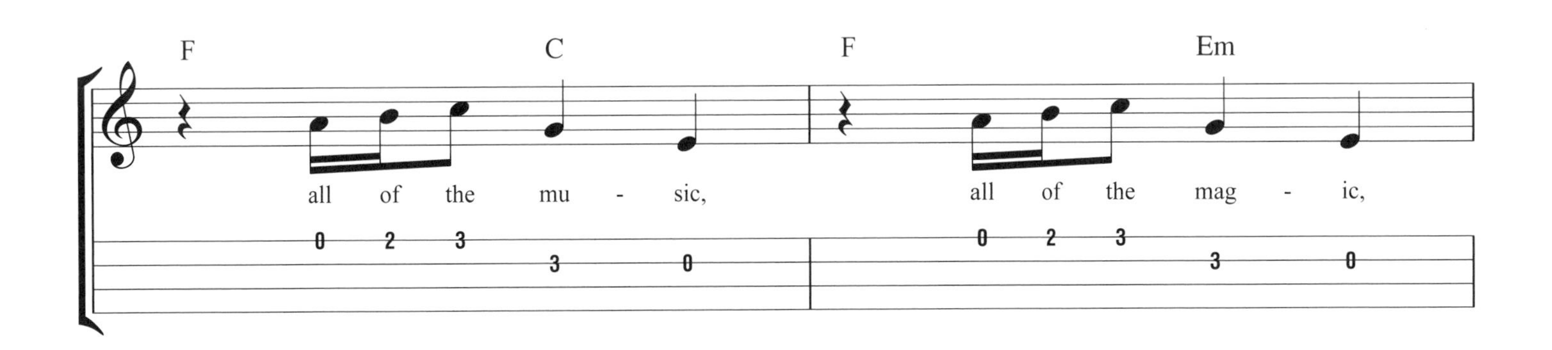
F C F Em
all of the mu - sic, all of the mag - ic,

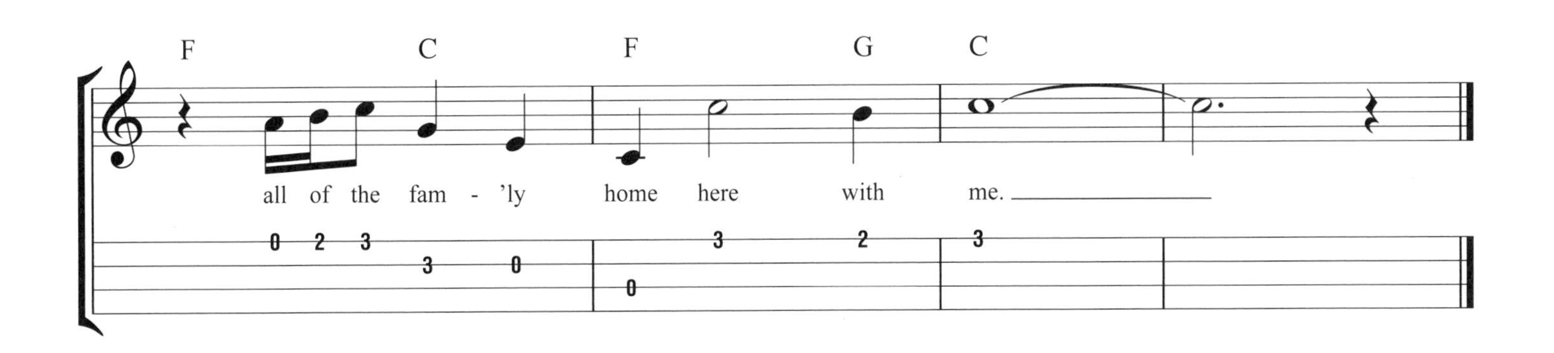
F C F G C
all of the fam - 'ly home here with me.

White Christmas

from the Motion Picture Irving Berlin's HOLIDAY INN

Words and Music by Irving Berlin

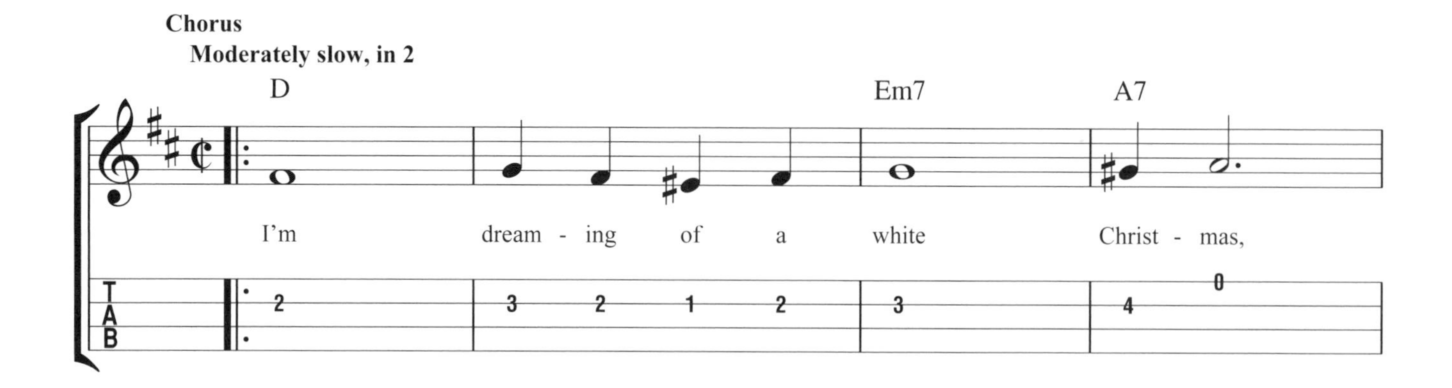

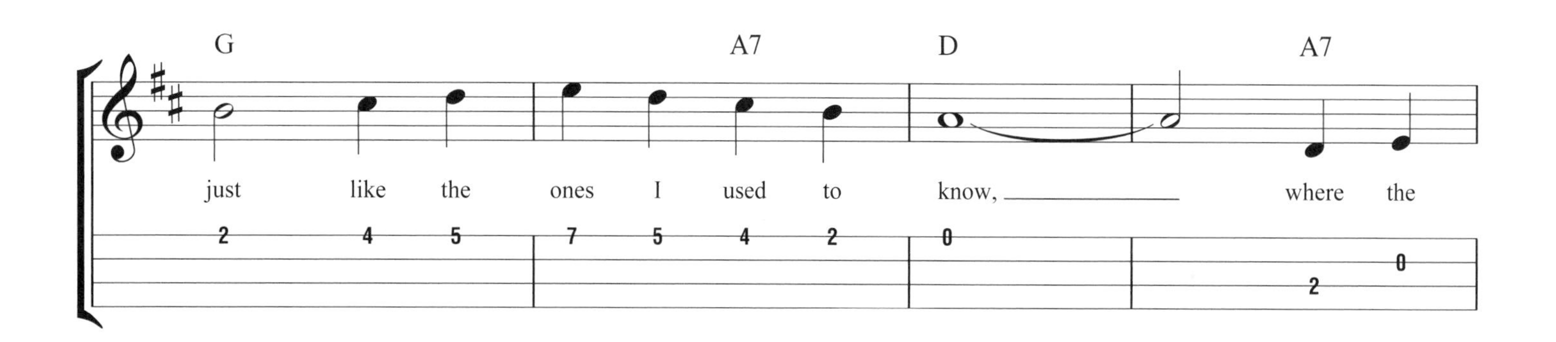

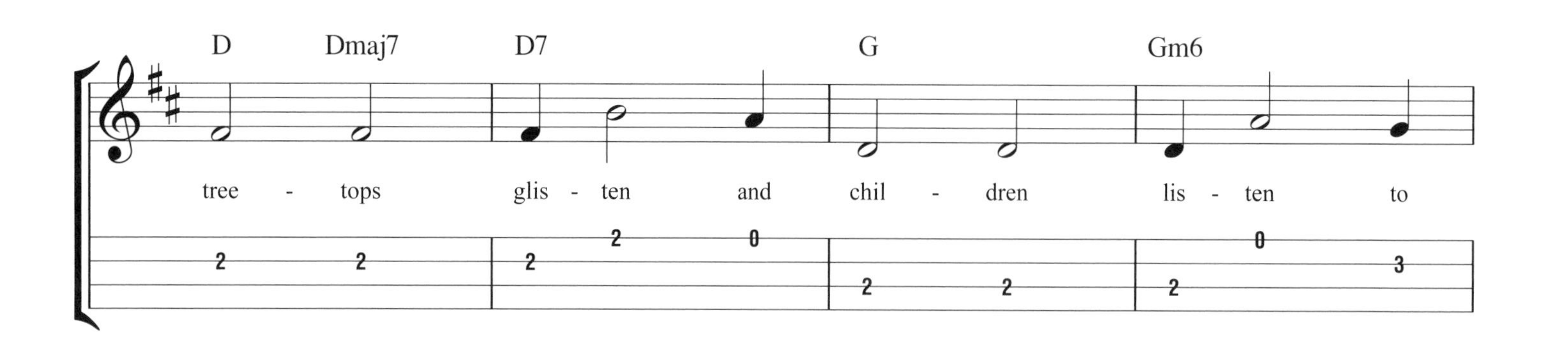

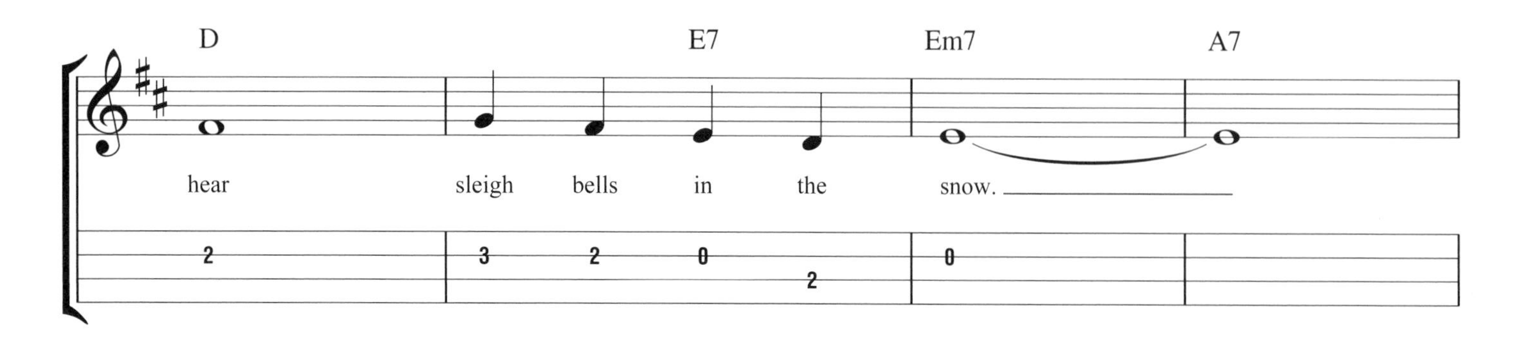

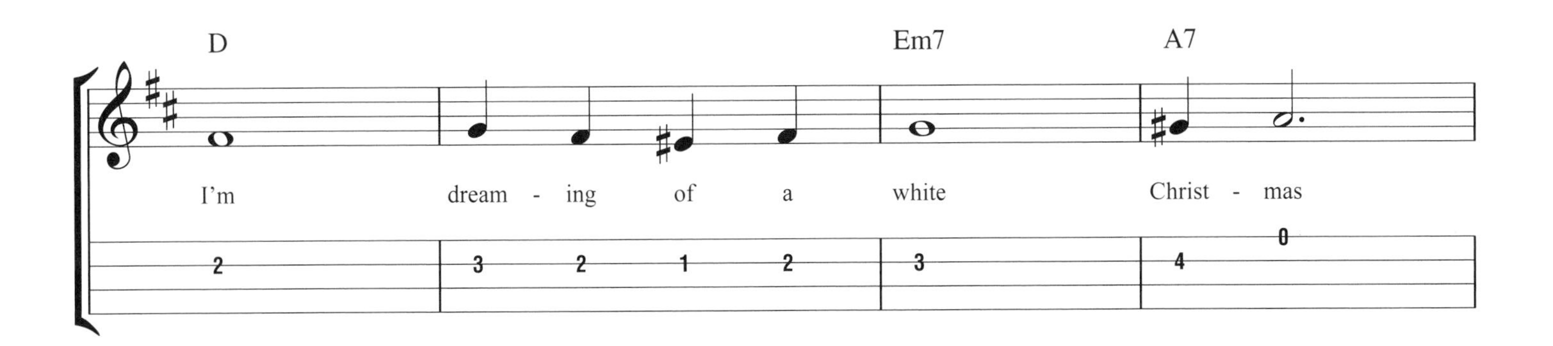
D Em7 A7
I'm dream - ing of a white Christ - mas

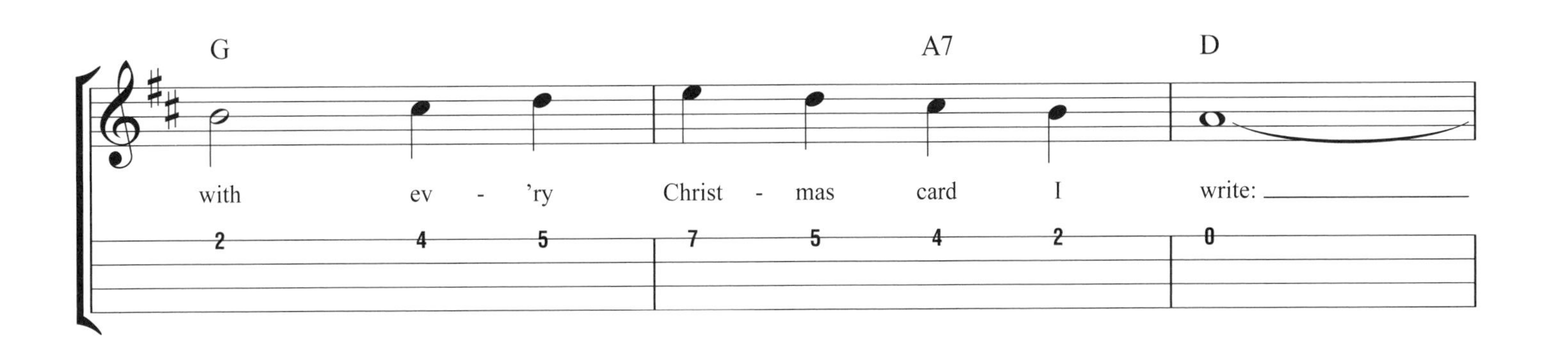
G A7 D
with ev - 'ry Christ - mas card I write:

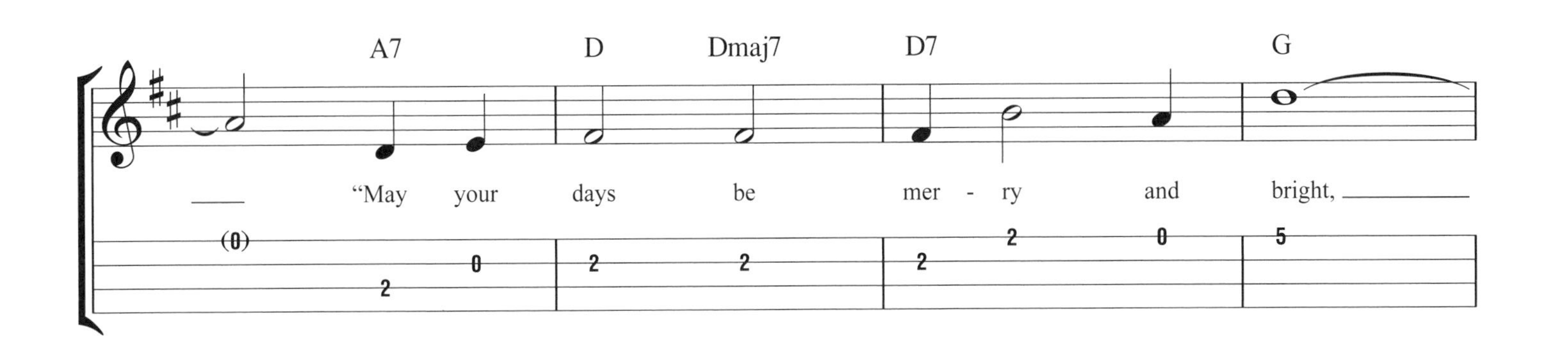
A7 D Dmaj7 D7 G
"May your days be mer - ry and bright,

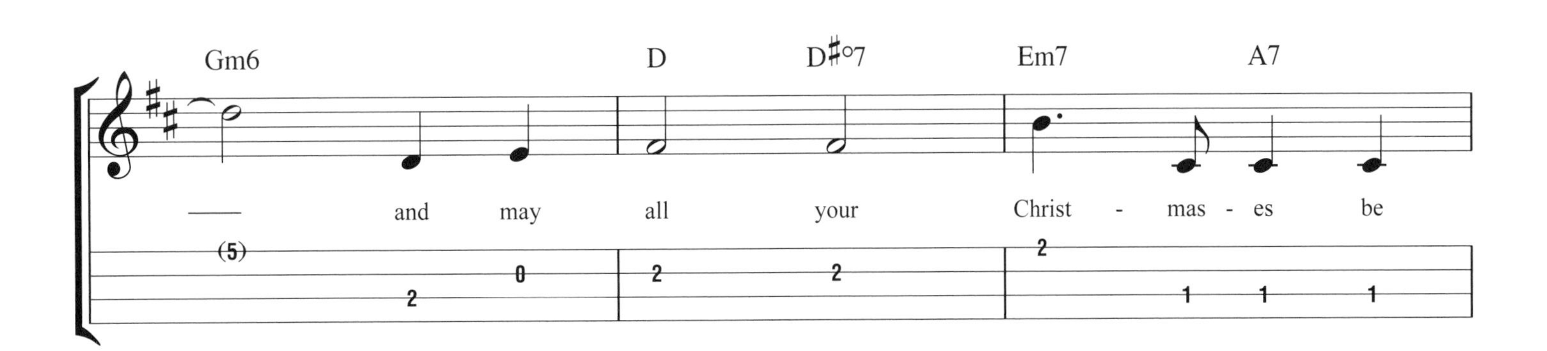
Gm6 D D♯°7 Em7 A7
and may all your Christ - mas - es be

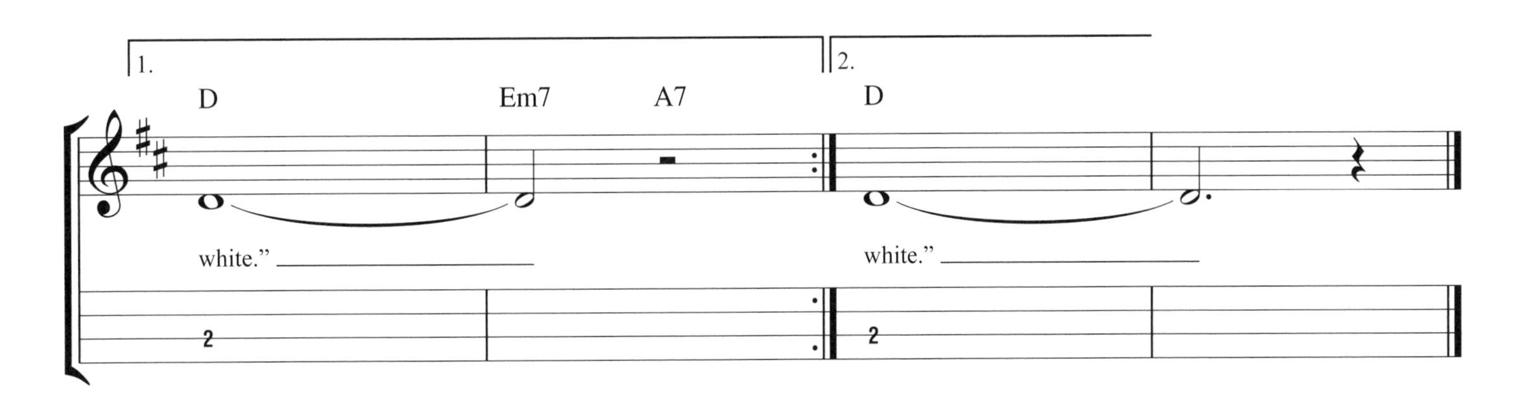
1. 2.
D Em7 A7 D
white." white."

You're All I Want for Christmas

Words and Music by Glen Moore and Seger Ellis

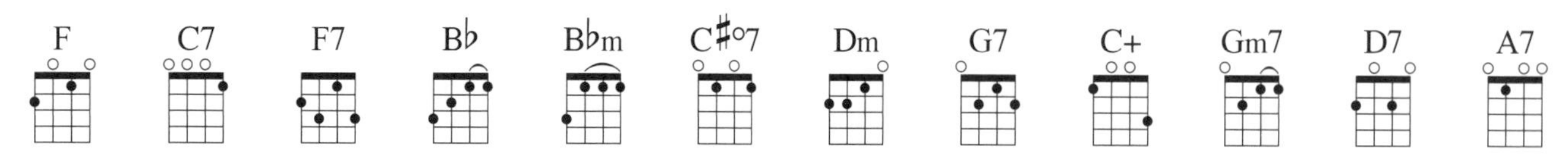

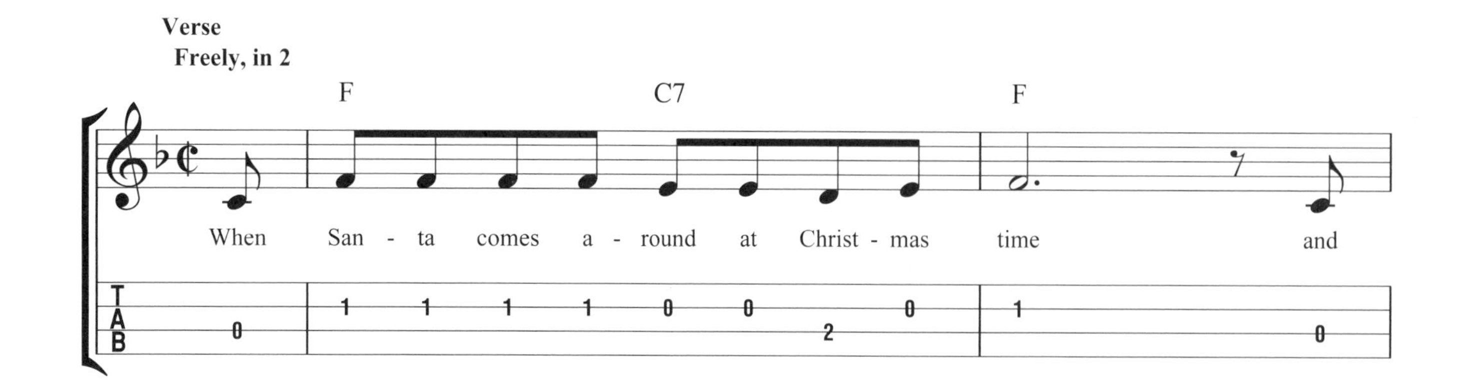

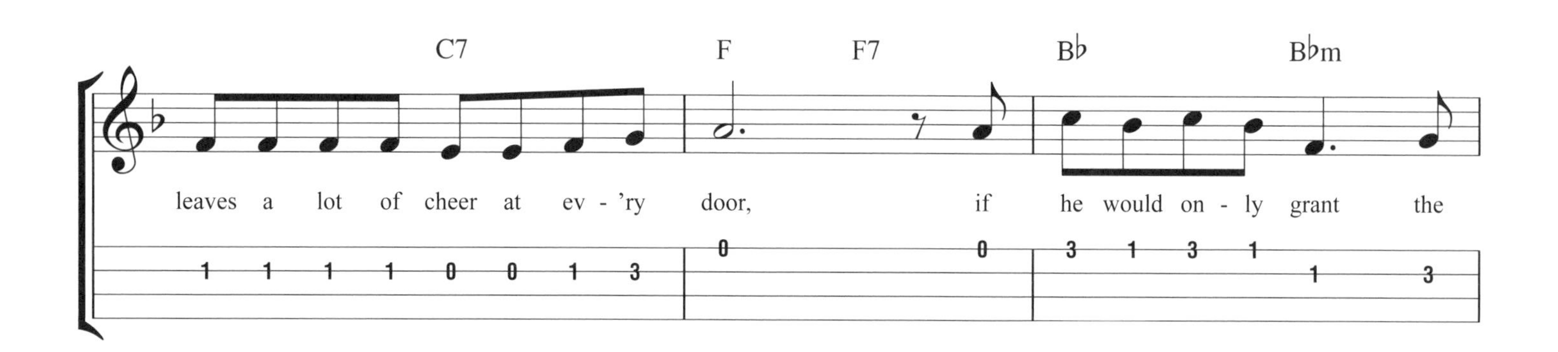

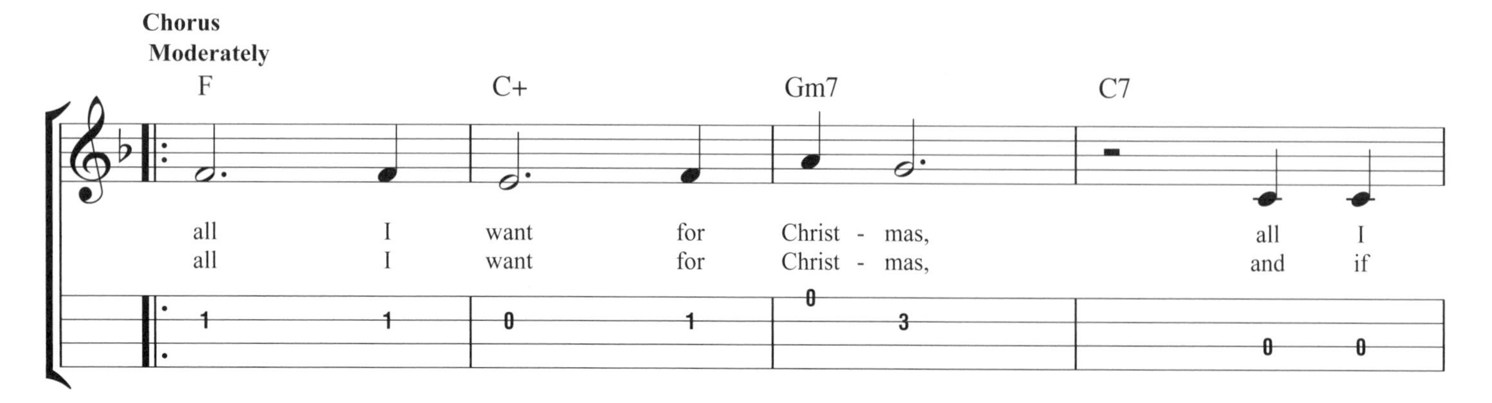

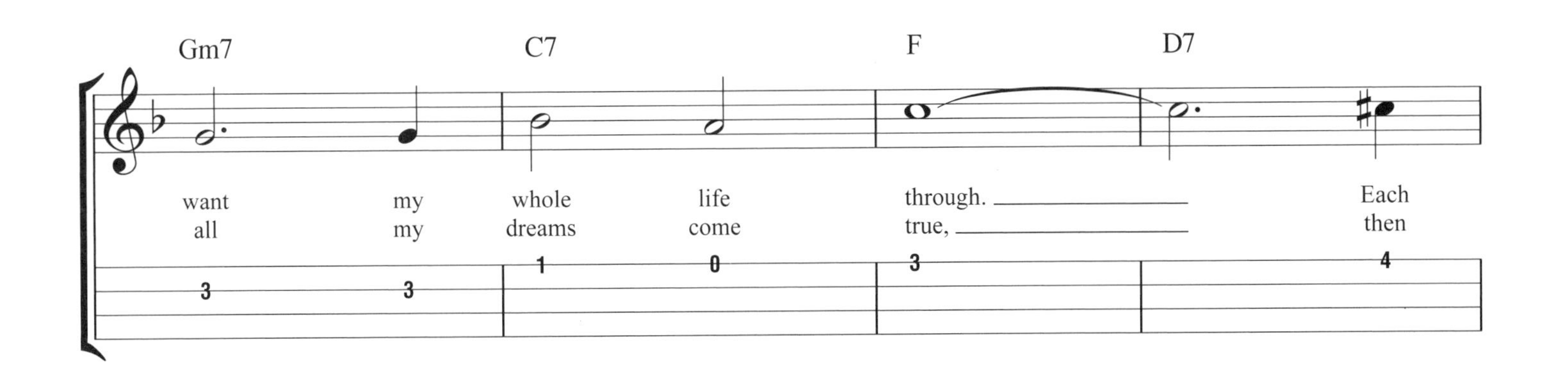
Gm7 C7 F D7
want my whole life through. Each
all my dreams come true, then

1.
Gm7 A7 Dm
day is just like Christ - mas an - y
I'll a -

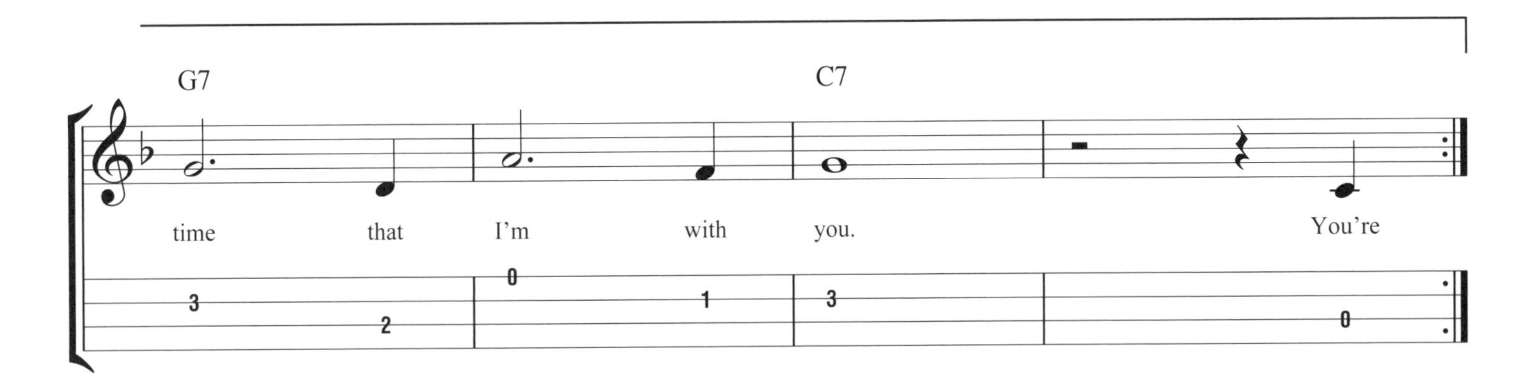
G7 C7
time that I'm with you. You're

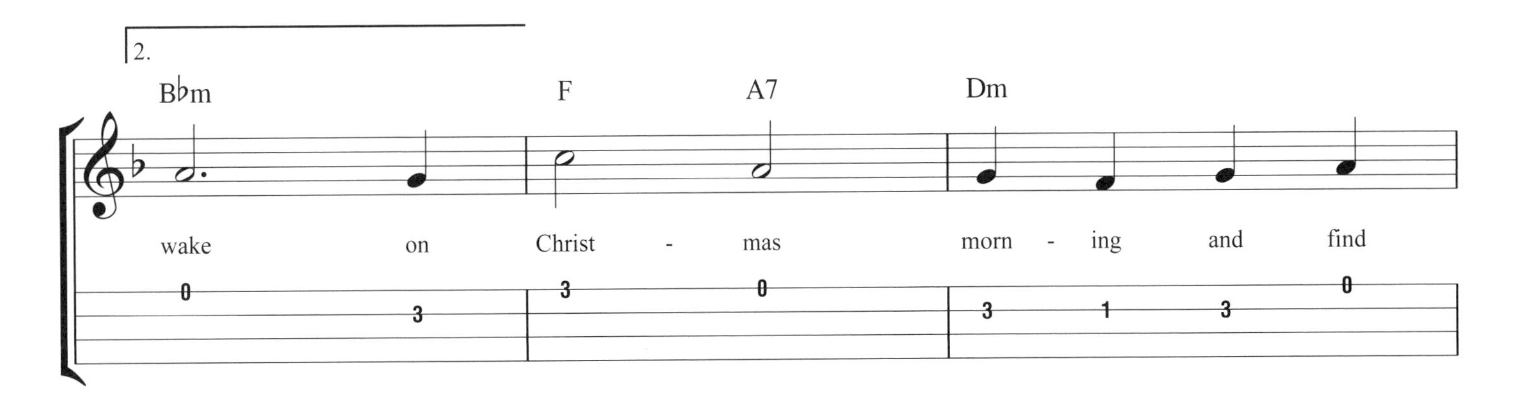
2.
B♭m F A7 Dm
wake on Christ - mas morn - ing and find

G7 C7 F B♭ F
my stock - ing filled with you.

Winter Wonderland

Words by Dick Smith
Music by Felix Bernard

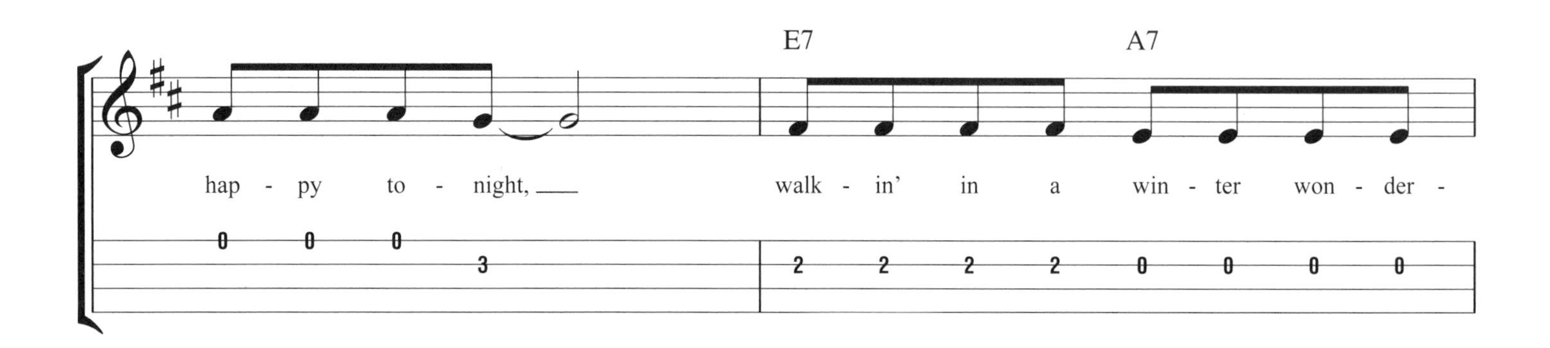

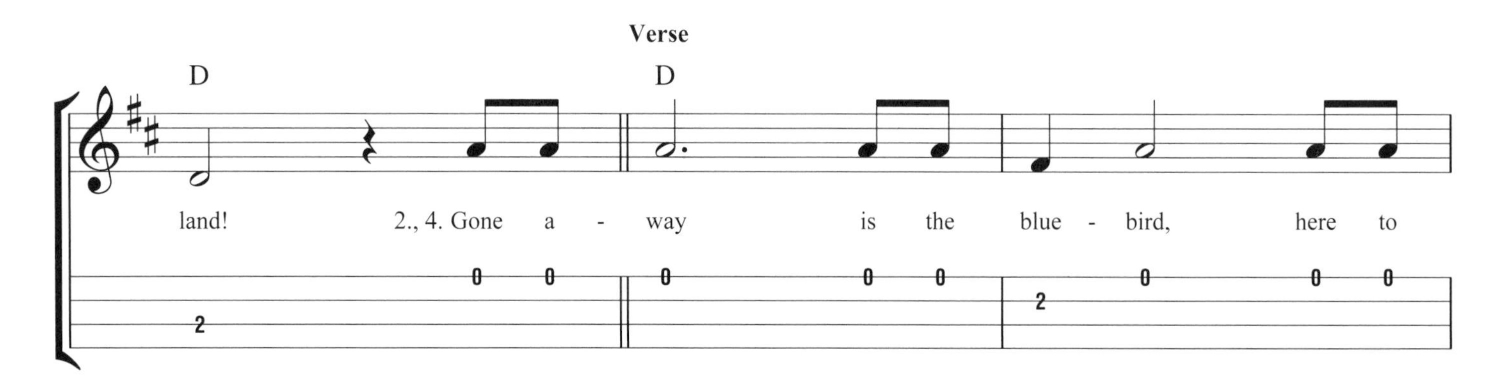

A7
stay is a new bird.
He sings a love song
He's sing - ing a song
as

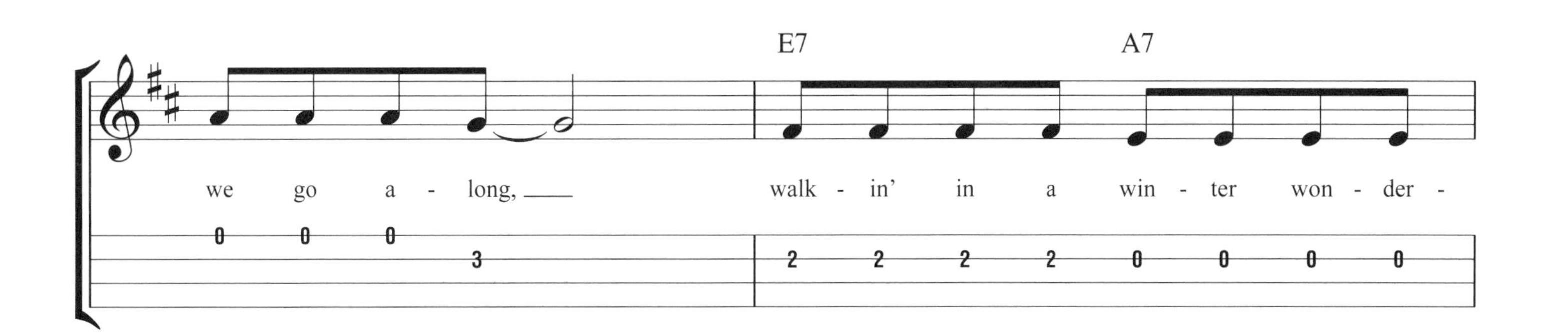
E7
A7
we go a - long,
walk - in' in a win - ter won - der -

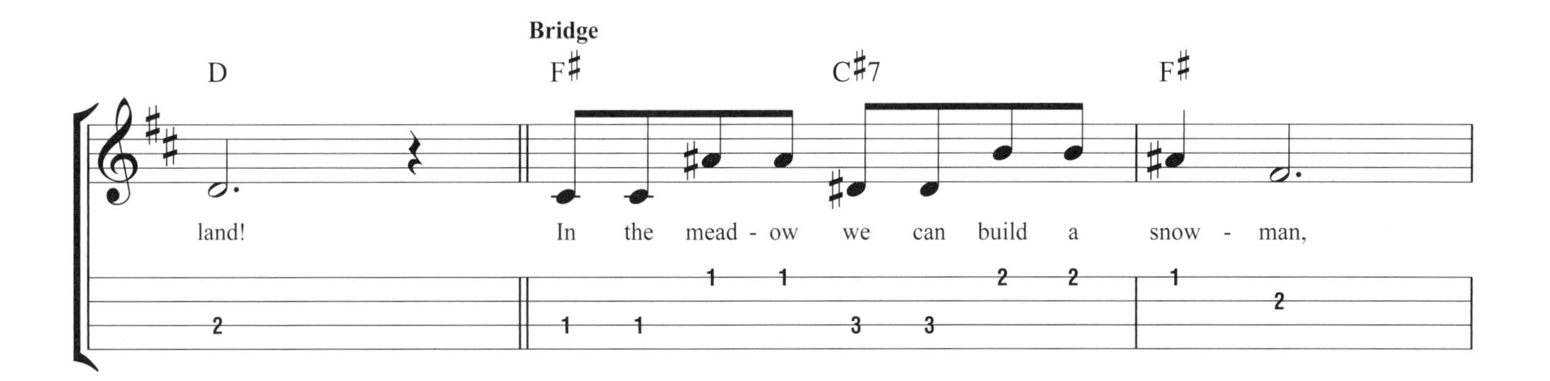
Bridge
D
F♯
C♯7
F♯
land!
In the mead - ow we can build a snow - man,

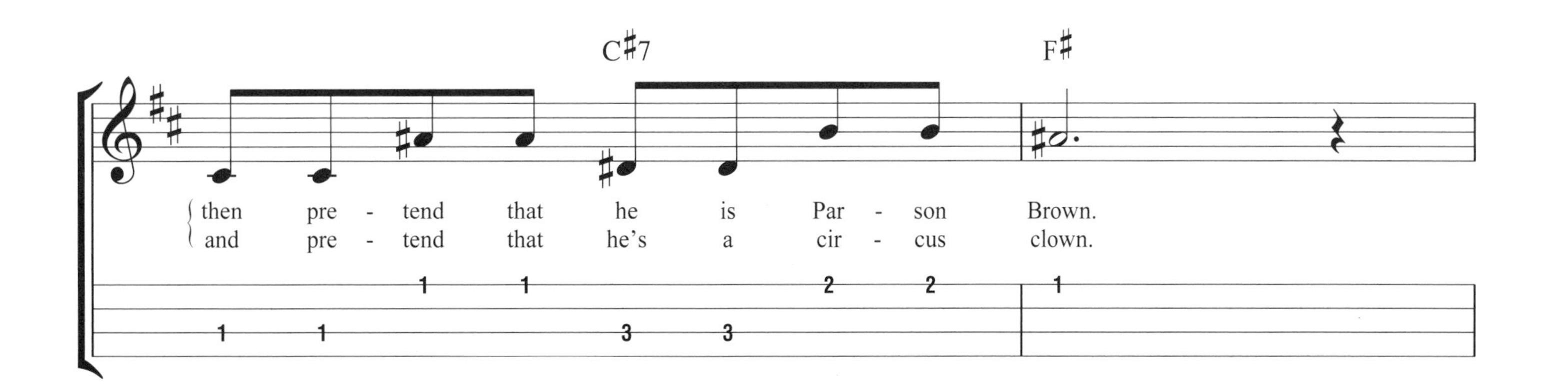
C♯7
F♯
then pre - tend that he is Par - son Brown.
and pre - tend that he's a cir - cus clown.

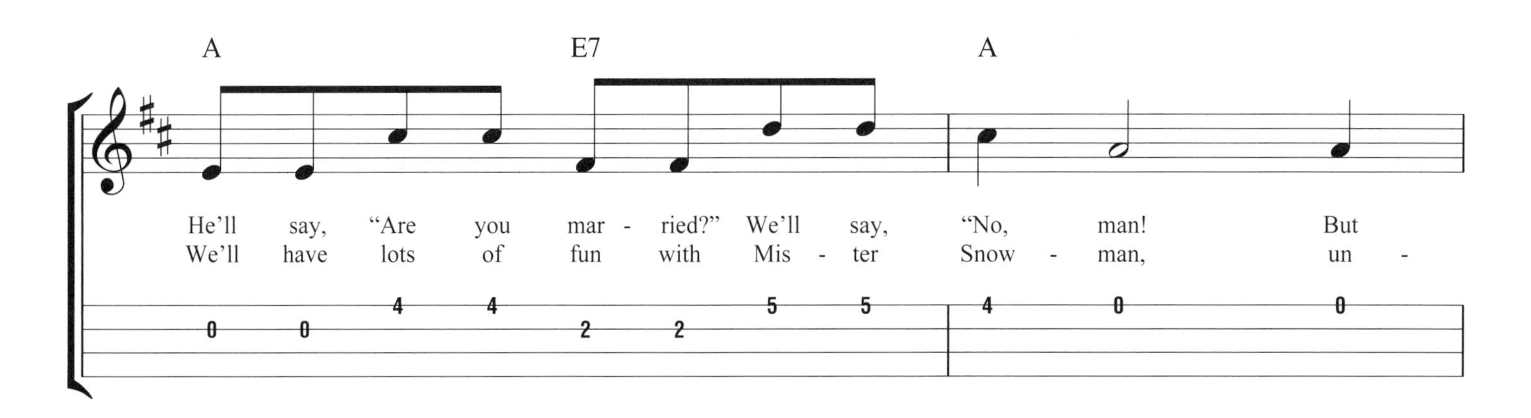
A
E7
A
He'll say, "Are you mar - ried?" We'll say, "No, man! But
We'll have lots of fun with Mis - ter Snow - man, un -

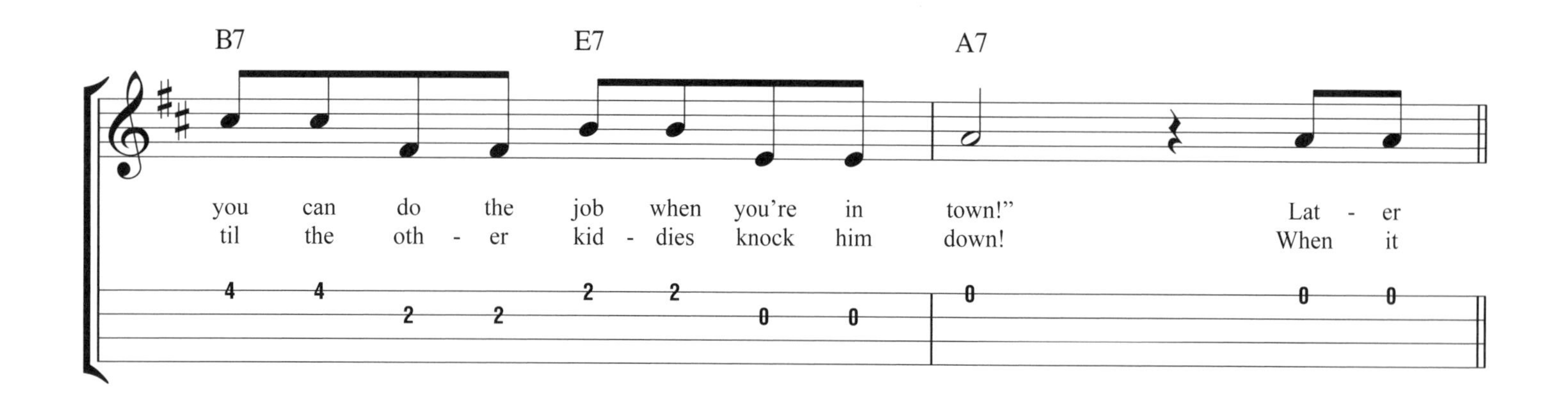
B7
E7
A7
you can do the job when you're in town!" Lat - er
til the oth - er kid - dies knock him down! When it

Outro-Verse

D
A7
on, we'll con - spi - re as we dream by the
snows, ain't it thrill - in', tho' your nose gets a

fi - re, to face un - a - fraid the
chill - in'? We'll frol - ic and play the

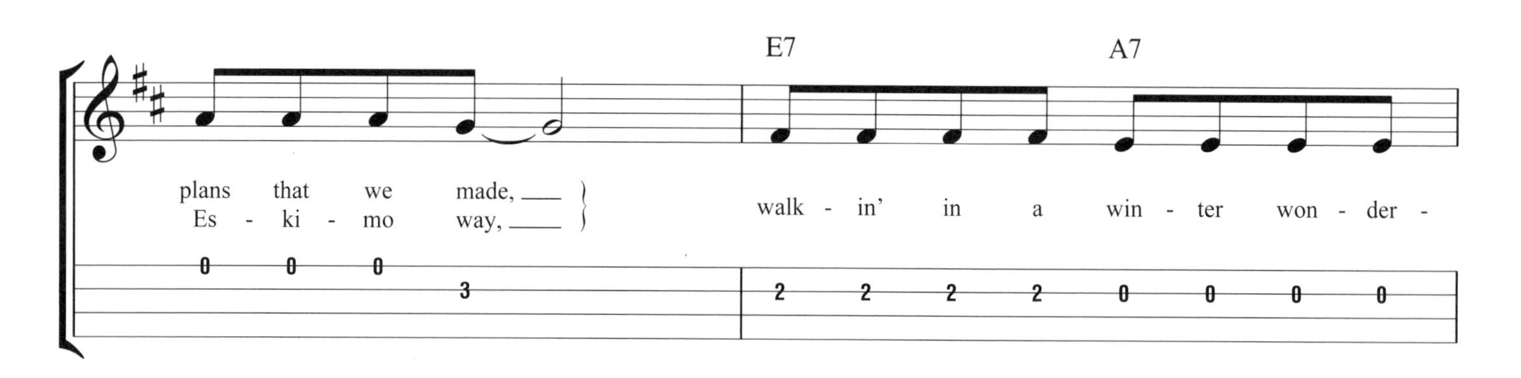
E7
A7
plans that we made,
Es - ki - mo way,
walk - in' in a win - ter won - der -

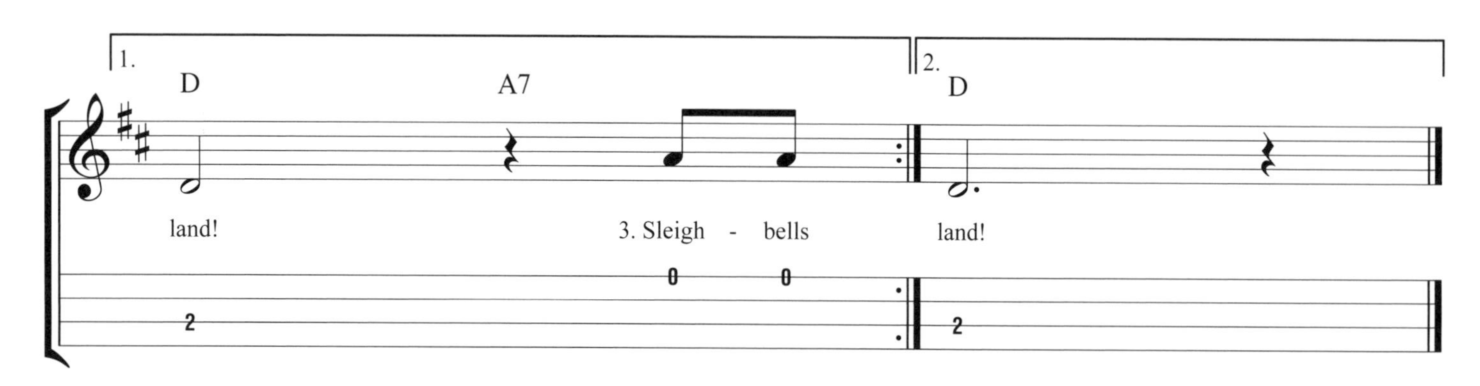
1.
2.
D
A7
D
land! 3. Sleigh - bells land!